Workbook

Living and Working in English

Joan Saslow

Workbook by

Barbara R. Denman

Workplace Plus: Living and Working in English 2
Workbook

Pearson Education, 10 Bank Street, White Plains, NY 10606

Vice president, publishing: Allen Ascher
Senior acquisitions editor: Marian Wassner
Development editors: Martin Yu and Peter Benson
Vice president, director of design and production: Rhea Banker
Executive managing editor: Linda Moser
Production editor: Christine Lauricella
Production supervisor: Liza Pleva
Director of manufacturing: Patrice Fraccio
Senior manufacturing buyer: Dave Dickey
Cover design: Ann France
Text design: Ann France
Text composition: Word & Image Design Studio Inc.
Illustrations: Crowleart Group, pp. 6, 62, 63,(top), 84; Brian Hughes, pp.9, 26, 32, 33, 47, 59, 63, 89, 97, 98; Suzanne Mogensen, pp.24, 35, 43, 53; NSV Productions, pp.22,65; Meryl Treatner, pp.1, 19, 57
Photography: Gilbert Duclos, pp.40, 56, 64, 72, 76

ISBN: 0-13-033182-1

Printed in the United States of America
4 5 6 7 8 9 10–BAH–07 06 05

Contents

Name ______________________ ID ____________ Date ____________

UNIT 1

Your life and work

Vocabulary

1 **Look at the pictures. Circle the letter.**

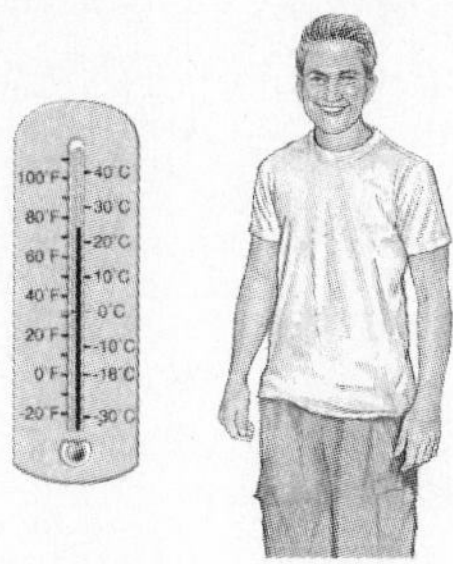

1. a. hot
   b. warm
   c. cold

2. a. cloudy
   b. sunny
   c. raining

3. a. breakfast
   b. lunch
   c. dinner

4. a. morning
   b. afternoon
   c. night

2 **CHALLENGE** **Look at the weather. What clothes do you need? Complete the chart. Use your own words.**

Raining	Cold	Hot

➤ Practical conversations

3 Put the conversation in order. Write the number on the line.

__1__ The Lunch Place. May I help you?

_____ Yes. And thank you.

_____ OK. This is Mia Chen.

_____ 555-6732?

_____ No, I'm sorry. She's not here right now.

_____ Oh. When will she be back?

_____ OK, Ms. Chen. And what's your number?

_____ Yes, please. Is Libby in?

_____ In about 30 minutes. Would you like to leave a message?

_____ It's (301) 555-6732.

__11__ You're welcome.

4 Complete the conversations. Use your <u>own</u> words.

1. **A:** Super Foods. Can I help you?

   B: Yes, please. Is Alta Morales there?

   A: ______________________. Who's calling, please?

   B: ______________________.

2. **A:** Hi, Tomas. What's it like outside?

   B: Oh, hi, Leslie. It's ______________________. By the way, are there any messages for me?

   A: ______________________.

Name ______________________ ID ____________ Date ____________

➤ Practical grammar

5 Complete the answers. Use will, 'll, or won't in your answers.

1. **A:** Will Ms. Rivas need the meeting room tomorrow?

   B: Yes, ______________________.

2. **A:** When will Clara cook dinner?

   B: ______________________ at 6:30 p.m.

3. **A:** What will your brother teach in Mali?

   B: ______________________ English.

4. **A:** When will the Cosaks pay for the car?

   B: ______________________ on Tuesday.

5. **A:** Will Ari and Stella meet us for lunch?

   B: No, ______________________. They have to work.

6 Look at the answers. Write questions.

1. **A:** When ____?

   B: Ellen will be back in the afternoon.

2. **A:** Where ____?

   B: Tonia will leave the paper in the supply room.

3. **A:** Who ____?

   B: Jiya and Ollie will cook lunch for the meeting.

4. **A:** Where ____?

   B: They'll eat dinner at their hotel.

5. **A:** When ____?

   B: I'll fix the time clock tomorrow morning.

7 Complete the conversations. Use words from the box.

me	you	him	her	us

1. **A:** We're going to go shopping tomorrow. Do you want to go with ________?
   (1.)

   B: Oh, I'm sorry. I can't. My brother is going to paint the house, and I want to help ________.
   (2.)

   A: Oh, OK. Is your sister going to help too?

   B: I don't know. I need to talk to ________.
   (3.)

2. **A:** Hi, Barry. By the way, Sam called ________ when you were at lunch.
   (4.)

   B: He did? Did he leave a message for ________?
   (5.)

   A: No, he didn't. He'll call back.

8 Complete the conversation. Use a form of would like to in your answers.

A: What would you like to do tomorrow night?

B: ____________________ have a nice dinner and watch a video.
(1.)

A: ____________________ go to a restaurant?
(2.)

B: No, I'd like to cook dinner.

A: OK. What ____________________?
(3.)

B: I'd like to cook chicken and rice.

A: Great!

9 Answer the questions. Use a form of would like to and your own words.

1. What would you like to do next year?

   ____

2. What would your family like to buy?

   ____

3. Where would you like to work? Why?

   ____

Name ____________________ ID ____________ Date ____________

➤ Authentic practice

10 Read. Choose your response. Circle the letter.

1. "I'm sorry. He's not in right now."

   a. I'm not sure. **b.** I'd like to leave a message.

2. "Did anyone call when I was out?"

   a. Yes. Mr. Chen called. **b.** Yes. I called Mr. Chen.

3. "Would you care to leave a message?"

   a. No, thanks. I'll call back. **b.** I'll tell him you called.

4. "What will the weather be like on Tuesday?"

   a. I like this weather. It's warm and sunny. **b.** It'll be warm and sunny.

5. "What do you think you'd like to have for breakfast?"

   a. I'd like to have breakfast at 8:30. **b.** I'd like to have eggs and coffee.

11 Complete the conversation. Choose the correct response. Write the letter on the line.

A: Hi, Lanie. Is it snowing outside?

B: ________ 1.

A: I like your coat.

B: ________ 2.

A: No, he's not in.

B: ________ 3.

A: Sure. Do you want to leave a message for him?

B: ________ 4.

A: OK. Enjoy the snow!

B: ________ 5.

a. Yes, please. Tell him I'll call him after lunch.

b. Yes, it is.

c. Thanks, Ella. I will.

d. OK, no problem. Can you give him the box?

e. Thanks, Ella. Is Augusto here? These papers are for him.

12 **Look at the weather map. Then complete the paragraph.**

California is a large state. The weather in Northern California is not the same as the weather in Southern California. Los Angeles is in Southern California. Today, the weather in Los Angeles will be ________________ and
1.

________________. It will rain today in
2.

________________ and ________________.
3. 4.

At Yosemite National Park, it will be

________________ and ________________.
5. 6.

It will be sunny in ________________
7.

and ________________.
8.

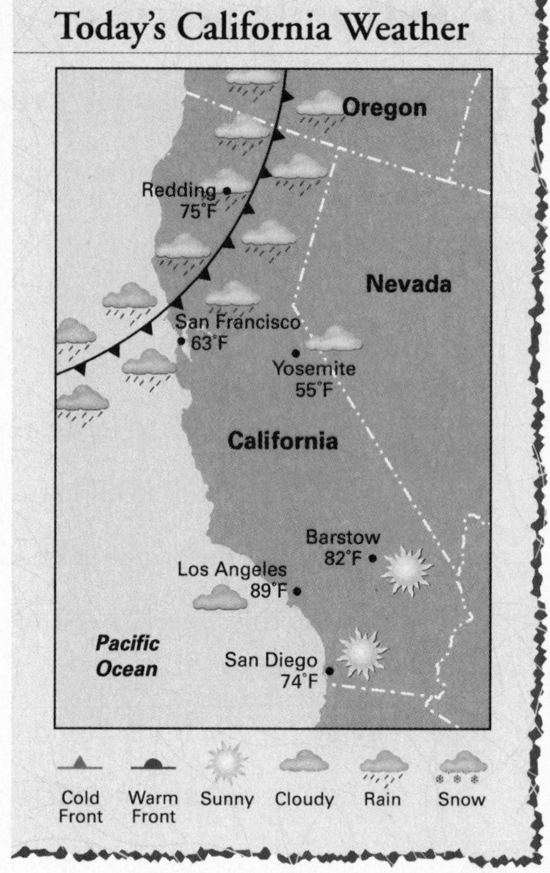

13 **Monica wants to do three things this week. She wants to go to the supermarket one day. She wants to wash her car one day. And she wants to stay home and study one day. Look at the weather for the next three days. Complete the sentences. Write your ideas for Monica.**

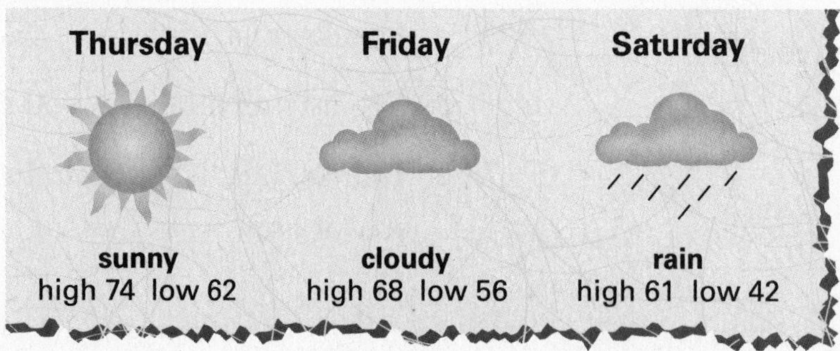

1. Go to the supermarket on ________________, because the weather will be ________________________________.

2. Wash your car on ________________, because the weather will be ________________________________.

3. Stay home and study on ________________, because ____.

Name ______________________ ID ____________ Date ____________

14 **Look at Gyorgi's date book for this week. Answer the questions. Use <u>will</u>, <u>'ll</u>, or <u>won't</u> in your answers.**

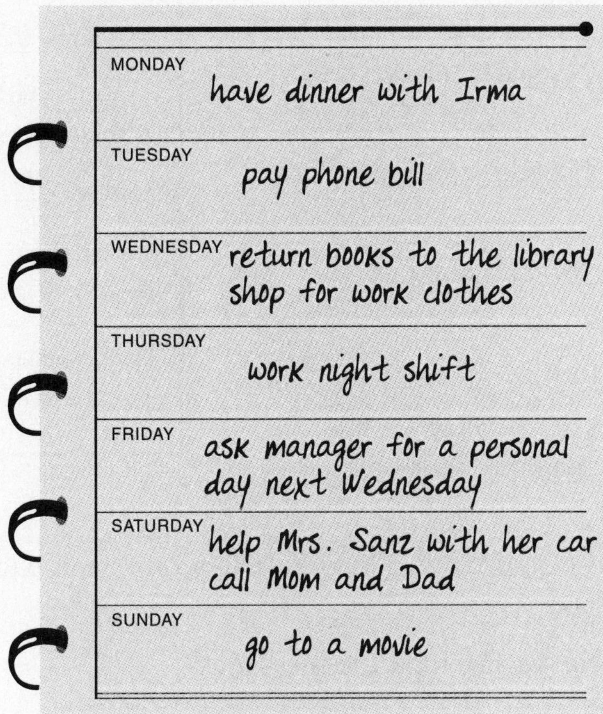

MONDAY
have dinner with Irma
TUESDAY
pay phone bill
WEDNESDAY
return books to the library
shop for work clothes
THURSDAY
work night shift
FRIDAY
ask manager for a personal day next Wednesday
SATURDAY
help Mrs. Sanz with her car
call Mom and Dad
SUNDAY
go to a movie

1. When will Gyorgi talk to his manager?
   He'll talk to his manager on Friday.
2. What will Gyorgi do on Wednesday?
   ____
3. Will Gyorgi call his mother and father on Sunday?
   ____
4. When will Gyorgi help Mrs. Sanz?
   ____
5. Will Gyorgi pay his phone bill this week?
   ____
6. Who will Gyorgi have dinner with?
   ____
7. Will Gyorgi go to a movie on Thursday?
   ____

15 **Look at the message form. Then read the paragraph. Circle the correct information.**

This telephone message is for (Mr. O'Brien / Mr. Nagaki).[1] (Mr. O'Brien / Mr. Nagaki)[2] called (Mr. O'Brien / Mr. Nagaki).[3] He called on (August 3 / March 8).[4] He called at (9:52 a.m. / 9:52 p.m.)[5] (Mr. O'Brien / Mr. Nagaki)[6] works at Capital Construction Company. (He will / He won't)[7] call back later. (Mr. O'Brien / Sylvie Nasta)[8] took the message.

To Jack O'Brien	
Date 8/3/02	Time 9:52 ☑ a.m. ☐ p.m.
WHILE YOU WERE OUT	
Mr Yoshi Nagaki	
From Capital Construction Company	
☑ telephoned	☐ please call
☐ returned your call	☑ will call back
Telephone number:	
Message taken by: Sylvie Nasta	

16 **Read the conversation. Then complete the message form. Use the date and time right now.**

YOU: Sun Tortillas. May I help you?

Mr. Ochoa: Yes, please. This is Aldo Ochoa from Mexico City Foods. Is Mr. Munoz in?

YOU: Mr. Munoz? No, I'm sorry. He's out of the office right now. Would you like to leave a message?

Mr. Ochoa: Yes, please. Please ask him to call me back.

YOU: And what is your number, Mr. Ochoa?

Mr. Ochoa: It's (201) 555-1653.

YOU: All right, Mr. Ochoa. I'll give him the message as soon as he gets back.

To ______	
Date ______	Time ______ ☐ a.m. ☐ p.m.
WHILE YOU WERE OUT	
M ______	
From ______	
☐ telephoned	☐ please call
☐ returned your call	☐ will call back
Telephone number: ______	
Message taken by: ______	

Name ______________________ ID ____________ Date ____________

UNIT 2

Your environment

Vocabulary

1 Look at the pictures. Write the words on the line.

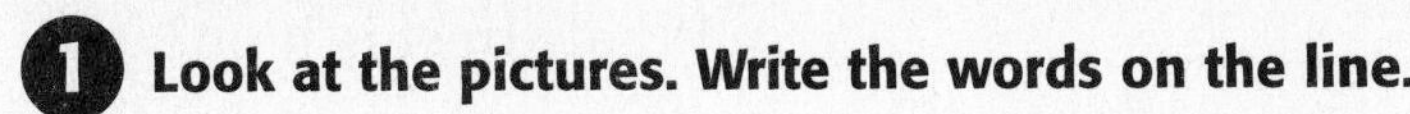

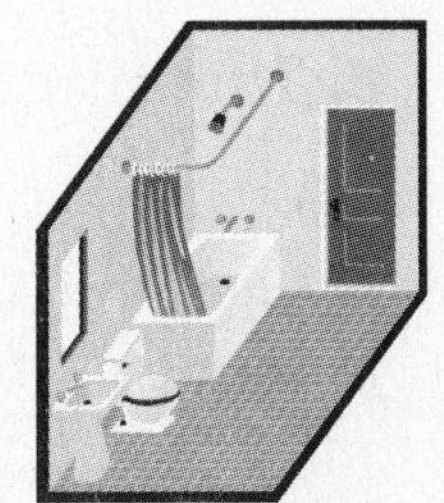

1. ____________________ 2. ____________________ 3. ____________________

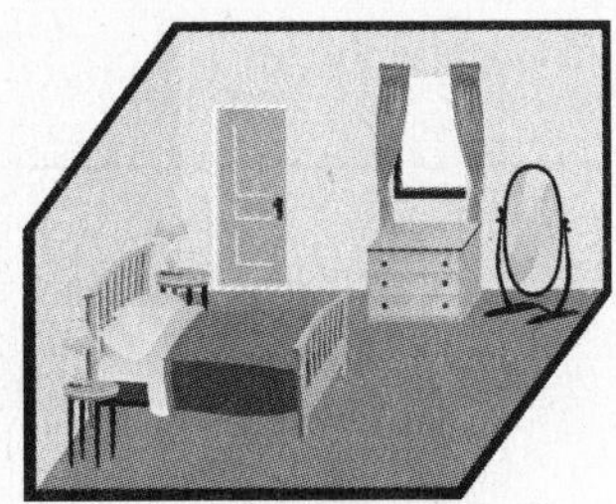

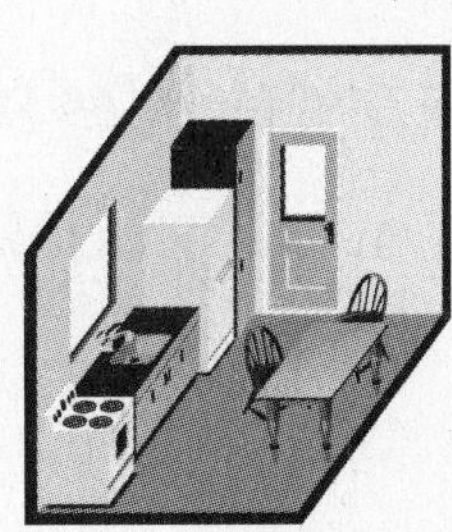

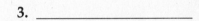

4. ____________________ 5. ____________________ 6. ____________________

2 Read the sentences. Match each sentence with a place. Write the letter on the line.

______	**1.** I need to take a bus.	**a.**	an elevator
______	**2.** We're going to wash our clothes.	**b.**	a subway station
______	**3.** Peter wants to buy food at 1:00 a.m.	**c.**	a laundry room
______	**4.** Moya's taking the subway to work.	**d.**	a bus station
______	**5.** I want to go to the 12th floor.	**e.**	a convenience store

➤ Practical conversations

3 Complete the conversation. Use words from the box.

across	month	rent	nearby	apartment	bedroom	right

A: There's an apartment for ______________ in my neighborhood.
1.

B: Really? I'm looking for an ______________. What street is it on?
2.

A: It's on First Street. It's ______________ from the park.
3.

B: How many bedrooms does it have?

A: It has one ______________, I think.
4.

B: Is there a bus stop ______________?
5.

A: Yes, there is. It's ______________ around the corner.
6.

B: And how much is the rent?

A: It's $450 a ______________.
7.

4 Complete the conversations. Use the map and your <u>own</u> words.

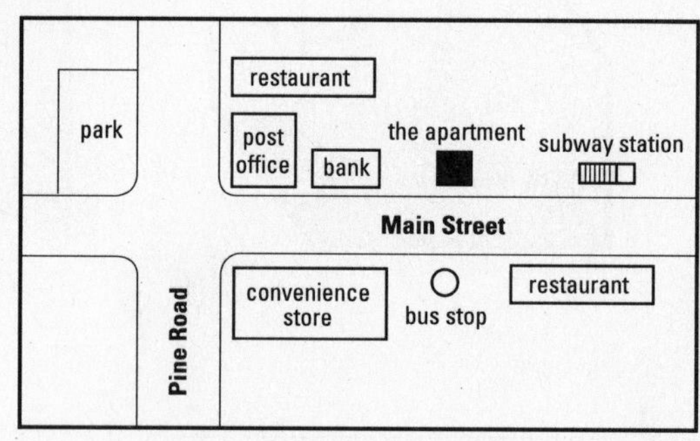

1. **A:** This apartment is nice. How much is the rent?

   B: ______________. The security deposit is ______________.

   A: Is there a ______________ nearby?

   B: Yes, there is. It's ______________.

2. **A:** What is the neighborhood like?

   B: Well, there's a ______________ nearby.

   A: Where is it?

   B: It's ______________.

Name ______________________ ID ______________ Date ______________

➤ Practical grammar

5 **Complete the conversations. Use it or them.**

1. A: Did you pay the water bill?

   B: Yes, I did. I paid __________ yesterday.

2. A: Where is the lease?

   B: I don't know. I don't have __________.

3. A: There are two nice apartments on the third floor.

   B: Can we see __________?

4. A: The security deposit is one month's rent.

   B: When do I have to pay __________?

5. A: Where are the people in apartment 2A from?

   B: I'm not sure. I don't know __________.

6. A: Are there two bus stops on this street?

   B: Yes, there are. You can see __________ from the apartment.

6 **Complete the conversations. Use object pronouns from the box.**

me	you	us	him	her	it	them

1. A: The Yesenis are looking for an apartment.

   B: Are you helping __________ (1.)?

   A: Yes, I am.

   B: There's an apartment for rent on my street. It's in the basement, in Mr. Wu's house.

   A: I don't know Mr. Wu. Can you give __________ (2.) his telephone number?

   B: I don't have __________ (3.). But I can give __________ (4.) his address.

   A: OK. I'll see Mr. Yeseni tomorrow. I can give __________ (5.) the address.

2. A: We would like to see the apartment. Can you show it to __________ (6.)?

   B: My wife has the keys. I'll call __________ (7.). She can show it to you.

7 **Read the sentences. Choose the correct answer. Circle the letter.**

1. Dina took a message. She gave it to Carol. Who has the message now?

   a. Dina has the message now. b. Carol has the message now.

2. We had a nice dinner at Olaf's house. He cooked it for us. Who cooked the dinner?

   a. Olaf cooked the dinner. b. We cooked the dinner.

3. Miki saw two apartments. The rental manager showed them to her. What did the rental manager show Miki?

   a. He showed her an apartment. b. He showed her two apartments.

4. Mehmet didn't clean the kitchen. Fernando cleaned it for him. What did Fernando do?

   a. He cleaned the kitchen. b. He didn't clean the kitchen.

8 **Write sentences with two object pronouns.**

1. Please give the security deposit to Mrs. Abbott.

   Please give it to her.

2. Can you install the computer for Mr. Tinh?

   ____

3. Please give this message to your mother and father.

   ____

4. I'll ask Mrs. Escobar for the lease.

   ____

5. I'd like to rent the house to the Zlatovs.

   ____

6. Will you paint the apartment for my wife and me?

   ____

9 **➤CHALLENGE** **Complete each sentence with two object pronouns. Use your own words.**

1. Mr. Kemper would like to see these letters. Please *give them to him.*
2. I don't have my glasses. I can't read these ads. Please ______________
3. My sister can't pay her electric bill. I ______________
4. We'd like to see the apartments now. Can you ______________

Name ______________________ ID ______________ Date ______________

➤ Authentic practice

10 Read. Choose your response. Circle the letter.

1. "We have a couple of one-bedrooms."
   a. Can I give it to you tonight? b. Can you show them to me?
2. "The rent is $550 per month."
   a. How much is the rent? b. What about utilities?
3. "When would you like to see the townhouse?"
   a. Is tomorrow OK? b. Yes. Tomorrow is OK.
4. "Do you want to look at the lease?"
   a. Yes, please. I'd like to show it to my husband. b. Yes. Please read it to me carefully.
5. "This building has a no-pet policy."
   a. No problem. b. Is that OK?

11 Complete the conversations. Choose words from the box.

neighborhood	deposit	lease	corner	electric

1. A: What about public transportation?
   B: There's a subway station just around the ________________.
2. A: What is the ________________ like?
   B: It's really nice. The people are friendly, and everyone knows everyone else.
3. A: Is the stove in the kitchen gas or ________________?
   B: I'm not sure. I'll have to check.
4. A: I'd like to see the ________________.
   B: Here you go. Please read it carefully. Let me know if you have any questions.
5. A: Do you require a security ________________?
   B: Yes, we do. It's $500.

12 **Read the sentences. Write the names on the buildings.**

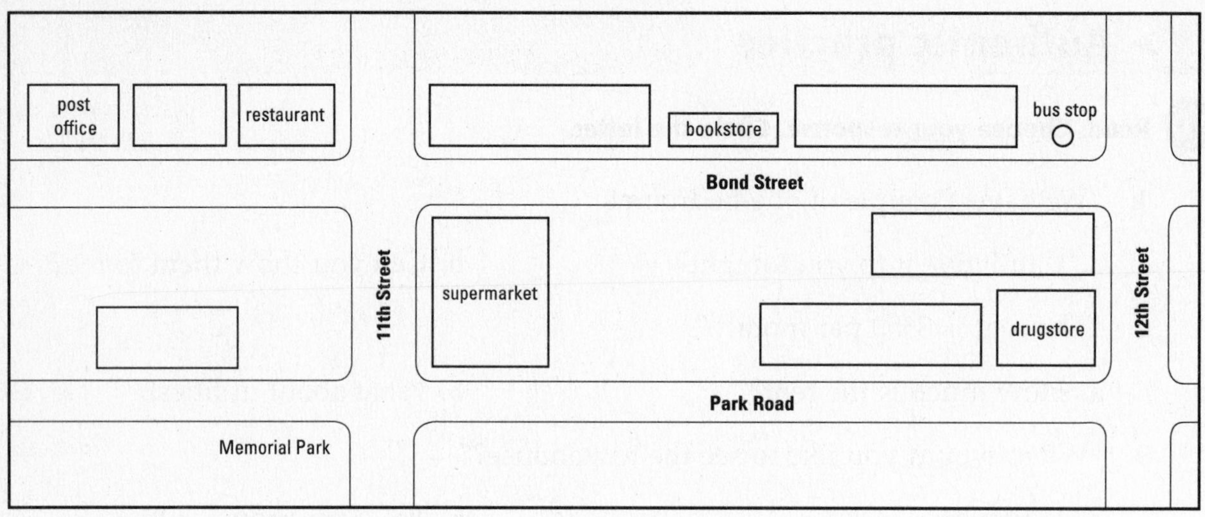

1. The convenience store is across the street from the bus stop.
2. The school is on Park Road, across the street from the park.
3. The subway station is across the street from the supermarket.
4. The parking lot is around the corner from the convenience store.
5. The bank is next door to the post office.
6. The doctor's office is down the street from the subway station.

13 **Read the ads and then fill in the chart.**

FOR RENT

Nice new apartment in CLAIRMONT
1 bed, 1 bth $550
we pay utilities
elevator building
free parking, no pets
(313) 555-7600

FOR RENT

MIDTOWN

3BR, 2BTH in small, older walk-up apartment building on quiet street. Near subway. New kitchen. $650/mo incl. utilities. Laundry room.

FOR RENT

EAST SIDE $575 + util
Large, sunny apartment in house. 2 bdrm, 2 bath
Near shopping and schools
Call Bettie at (826) 555-3741

FOR RENT

HILLSIDE
House 2BRs/1 Bath
Two parking spaces
Rent: $750/month
+ gas & electric
Call owner (405) 555-7392

City	Rent	Utilities included?	Bedrooms	Bathrooms
Hillside		no		
Clairmont				
Eastside			2	
Midtown		yes		

Name ______________________ ID ______________ Date ______________

14 **Look at Exercise 13 again. Then check ☑ yes, no, or I don't know.**

	yes	no	I don't know
1. You can keep a dog in the Clairmont apartment.	❑	❑	❑
2. You can wash your clothes in the Midtown apartment.	❑	❑	❑
3. There is an elevator in the Hillside apartment.	❑	❑	❑
4. You have to pay for parking in the Clairmont apartment.	❑	❑	❑
5. If you can pay only $575 a month, will you rent the Eastside apartment?	❑	❑	❑

15 **Look at the rental form. Then check ☑ true or false.**

Perry Rental Company — Rental Form

Name(s): *Tirsit Hagos/Solomon Alemu*

Date: *5/2* Phone: *(310) 555-3792*

Current Address: *1921 Lakeview Dr. Apt 3C*

Bayside, CA 90245

City or location: 1st choice *Bayside* 2nd choice *El Segundo*

Housing desired: ❑ house ☑ apartment ❑ room in house

No. of bedrooms: *1* No. of bathrooms: *1* Maximum rent: *$525*

Check any other needs:

☑ parking (on-street OK) ❑ parking (off-street) ❑ laundry room

❑ pets OK ❑ near bus/subway ❑ elevator

	true	false
1. Tirsit and Solomon are looking for an apartment.	❑	❑
2. They can pay $550 a month for the rent.	❑	❑
3. Tirsit and Solomon live in Bayside now.	❑	❑
4. They would like to rent another apartment in Bayside.	❑	❑
5. Tirsit and Solomon need one bedroom and one bathroom.	❑	❑
6. They need to rent a home near a bus stop.	❑	❑
7. Tirsit and Solomon have a dog.	❑	❑
8. They can park on the street.	❑	❑

16 **Read about the Chungs. Then complete the rental information form for them. Use today's date.**

Albert and Wei Chung are looking for a new place to rent. They live in an apartment now, but it's too small for them. They would like to rent a small house. Right now, Mr. and Mrs. Chung live in Crofton. Their address is 618 Ford Street, apartment 152. Their phone number is (419) 555-4792. They would like to find a house to rent in Crofton, but Waterside is OK for them too.

The Chungs have two sons, so they want a house with two bedrooms. They only need one bathroom. They have a car, but they don't want to park it on the street. Their children need to be able to take a city bus to school. The family has a dog.

Perry Rental Company — **Rental Form**

Name(s): ______________________

Date: ______________ Phone: ______________

Current Address: ______________________

Crofton, Ohio 43610

City or location: 1st choice ______________ 2nd choice ______________

Housing desired: ❑ house ❑ apartment ❑ room in house

No. of bedrooms: ________ No. of bathrooms: ________ Maximum rent: ________

Check any other needs:

❑ parking (on-street OK) ❑ parking (off-street) ❑ laundry room

❑ pets OK ❑ near bus/subway ❑ elevator

Name ______________________ ID ____________ Date ____________

UNIT 3

Your equipment and machines

Vocabulary

1 Complete the sentences. Write the letters of each word on the lines.

1. Alan had an accident. He had to call a t o w t r u c k.
2. When you drive at night, you have to turn on your h __ __ __ __ __ __ __ __ s.
3. You can put your shopping bags in the t __ __ __ k of my car.
4. Look! It's snowing! Do you need the windshield w __ __ __ __ __ s?
5. I want to check the engine. Can you open the h __ __ d?
6. We need to buy four new t __ __ __ s for the van.
7. Next to the gas pedal is the b __ __ __ e p __ __ __ l.
8. We don't need to buy g __ __. I filled it up yesterday.

2 Complete the sentences. Write the letter on the line.

1. One headlight is not working. I need to ______.
2. You can't park your car here. Please ______.
3. I have your new books. When can I ______?
4. These tires are very old. We need to ______.
5. You can't drive those cars. You'll need a tow truck to ______.
6. Your keys are in my office. Do you want to ______?

a. remove it
b. pick them up
c. replace them
d. drop them off
e. remove them
f. replace it

➤ Practical conversations

3 Complete the conversation. Use words from the box.

estimate	go on	drop off	signal	call
check	drop it off	problem	making	

A: A-1 Repair Shop. Can I help you?

B: Yes. This is Micha Bronski. I'd like to ________________ my car. Can you
1.

________________ it today?
2.

A: Yes, we can. What's the ________________?
3.

B: The turn ________________ won't ________________, and the engine is
4. 5.

________________ a funny sound.
6.

A: OK. Can you ________________ this morning?
7.

B: Sure. When can you give me an ________________?
8.

A: I'll give you a ________________ at noon.
9.

B: Great.

4 Complete the conversation. Use your own words.

A: I need a new truck!

B: Why? What's the problem?

A: My old truck is terrible. The ________________ won't ________________.

B: That's too bad. Anything else?

A: Well, yesterday the ______________________________ making a funny sound.

And today, the ______________________________ went on.

B: Did you get an estimate from your mechanic?

A: Yes. It was ______________________________! That's too expensive!

B: You don't need a new truck. You need a new mechanic!

Name ______________________ ID ______________ Date ______________

Practical grammar

5 **Complete the sentences. Use the two-word verbs from the box. Use it or them.**

drop off	turn on	pick up	fill up	turn off

1. The repair shop called, and they fixed the VCR. I'd like to _pick it up_ tonight.
2. We don't need the headlights now. I'm going to ______________.
3. Maya and Emmy need to go to school now. Can you ______________?
4. I need to put water in this bottle. Where can I ______________?
5. We want to use the coffee maker. How do we ______________?
6. We need eggs and milk. After work, can you ______________?

6 ***CHALLENGE*** **Look at the words and the picture. Write a sentence. Write what the person was doing. Use the past continuous.**

1. At 7:00 p.m. yesterday — Mr. Sanchez — the restroom

   At 7:00 p.m. yesterday, Mr. Sanchez was cleaning the restroom.

2. Last night at 11:00 p.m. — Petra — English

____

3. On Monday at 3:00 p.m. — my friends and I — coffee

____

4. At 10:30 yesterday morning — Mr. Wosczyk — a car

____

5. At 8:00 a.m. today — Greta — the bedroom

____

6. When I called — Ms. Kim — a customer's hair

____

7 **Circle the correct word or words to complete the sentence.**

1. I (had / was having) lunch when Sandy (called / was calling).
2. I (drove / was driving) home when it (started / was starting) to rain.
3. I (worked / was working) in a restaurant when I (met / was meeting) Nina.
4. Olaf (replaced / was replacing) his engine when he (hurt / was hurting) his back.
5. We (walked / were walking) to the subway station when an ambulance (came / was coming) to the bank.

8 **Complete the paragraph with the past continuous or the simple past tense of the verb. Write the verb on the line.**

I ____________ (1. go) to the store last night when it ____________ (2. start) to snow. When I ____________ (3. turn off) the lights at 11:30, it ____________ (4. snow). This morning at 6:30, when I ____________ (5. look) outside, it ____________ (6. snow). When I ____________ (7. turn on) the radio, the weatherman ____________ (8. give) the weather report. It's going to snow for three days!

9 **Answer the questions with the past continuous. Use your own words.**

1. What were you doing at 7:00 this morning?

   ____

2. What were you doing at noon yesterday?

   ____

3. What were you doing at 10 p.m. last night?

   ____

Name ______________________ ID ______________ Date ______________

Authentic practice

10 **Read. Choose your response. Circle the letter.**

1. "When can I call for the estimate?"

   a. At 4:00 p.m. b. $40.00.

2. "Was the brake light working when you drove the car yesterday?"

   a. No, it didn't. b. No, it wasn't.

3. "Can you look at this old lawn mower? It's making a funny sound."

   a. Did you remove the engine? b. Did you check the engine?

4. "The van needs gas. The gauge is on 'E'."

   a. OK. I'll fill it up tomorrow. b. OK. I'll pick it up tomorrow.

5. "Is 7:30 good for you?"

   a. Yes. Can you pick me up? b. No. The clock isn't working.

11 **Put the conversation in order. Write the number on the line.**

__1__ Can I help you?

______ Sure. We'll give you a call.

______ OK. We can check them. Anything else?

______ Yes, thanks. I need to drop off this TV for service.

______ Can I get an estimate before you fix it?

______ What's the problem?

______ Yes. When I turn it on, I don't get a picture for two or three minutes.

______ Well, the volume and color buttons don't always work.

______ No picture. OK. We'll look at it.

__10__ Thanks.

12 Look at the owner's manual. Read the instructions.

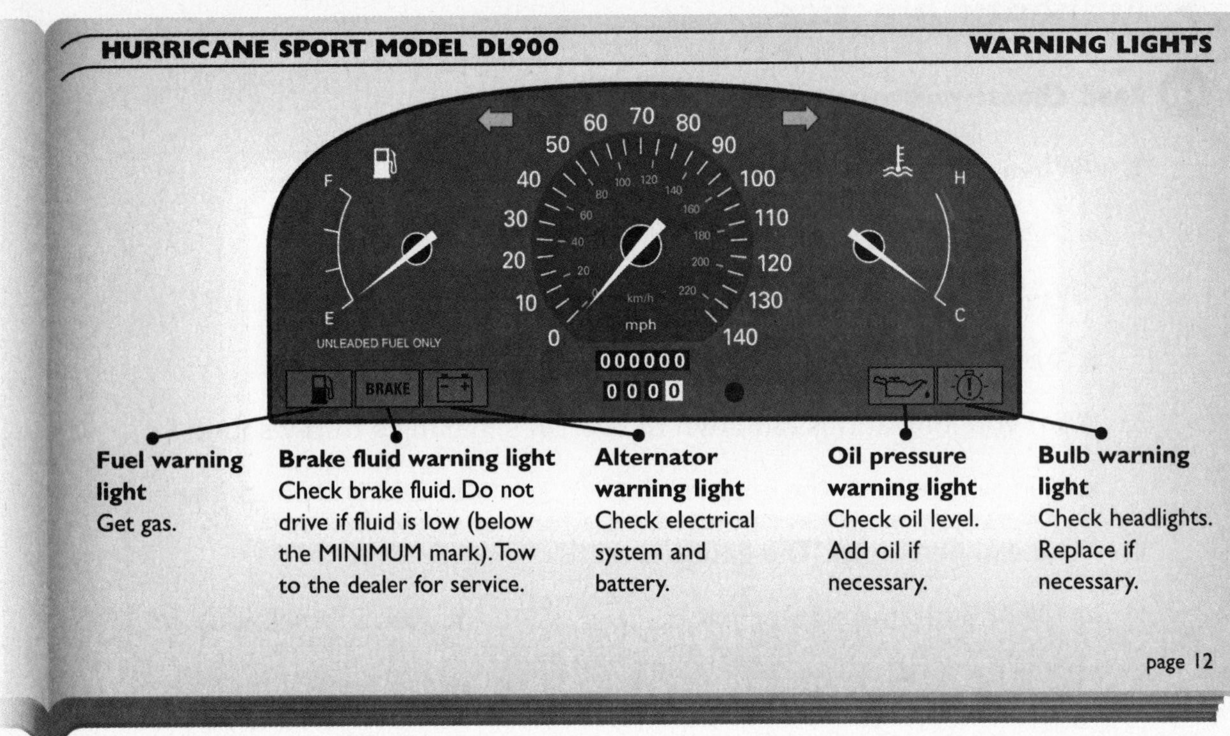

HURRICANE SPORT MODEL DL900
WARNING LIGHTS
F
E
UNLEADED FUEL ONLY
H
C
mph
km/h
BRAKE
Fuel warning light
Get gas.
Brake fluid warning light
Check brake fluid. Do not drive if fluid is low (below the MINIMUM mark). Tow to the dealer for service.
Alternator warning light
Check electrical system and battery.
Oil pressure warning light
Check oil level. Add oil if necessary.
Bulb warning light
Check headlights. Replace if necessary.
page 12

Complete the sentences. Match each item on the left with an item on the right. Write the letter on the line.

1. The alternator warning light comes on ______
2. The oil pressure warning light comes on ______
3. The bulb warning light comes on ______
4. The fuel warning light comes on ______
5. The brake fluid warning light comes on ______

a. when you need to fill the car with gas.

b. when a headlight isn't working.

c. if the brakes need fluid.

d. when you need to check the oil level.

e. when you need to check the battery.

Name ______________________ ID ______________ Date ______________

13 **Read the conversation. Then check ☑ true or false.**

Cho Hu: Oh no! The copier's out of order again.

Delia Cruz: Can you open it?

Cho Hu: Yes, but I can't see anything wrong.

Delia Cruz: So what's the problem?

Cho Hu: I don't know, but it won't start, and the warning light is on.

Delia Cruz: Which warning light?

Cho Hu: It's a little picture of a person.

Delia Cruz: Oh, that's the technician light. It means we have to call the service center. We can't repair it here.

Cho Hu: OK, I'll call.

	true	false
1. The copier isn't working.	☐	☐
2. The copier won't open.	☐	☐
3. A warning light came on.	☐	☐
4. They can fix the copier.	☐	☐
5. The warning light has a picture of a person.	☐	☐
6. Cho Hu is going to call the service center.	☐	☐

14 **Look at the conversation in Exercise 13 again. Complete the service center form. Use today's date and the time it is now.**

Describe the problem:

742

Ozzie's Office Machine Repair

Repair / Service Work Order

Machine: ☐ fax machine ☐ copier ☐ computer

Date of call:

Time of call:

Caller's name:

Warning light(s) on: ☐ yes ☐ no

If yes, check which warning light(s):

☐ toner ☐ paper ☐ door open

☐ paper jam ☐ technician

15 ➤ *CHALLENGE* **Read the night drop-off policy. Then complete the paragraph.**

Service Forms and Envelopes

Night Drop-Off Slot

NIGHT DROP-OFF POLICY

- If you need to drop your car off at night, please park your car in the parking lot next door. Don't park in front of the garage.
- Take a service form and envelope from the box near the door. Fill out the service form completely.
- Put your car key and the service form in the envelope and put them in the night drop-off slot.
- We will call you on the next work day and give you an estimate for your repairs. Thank you.

At Hernan's Garage, you can ________________ (1.) your car when the garage is closed at night. It's OK to park in the ________________ (2.). It's not OK to park ________________ (3.). Service forms and envelopes are in a ________________ (4.) near the door. First, ________________ (5.) a service form. Then put the form and your ________________ (6.) in an envelope and put it in the night drop-off slot. The mechanics will give you an ________________ (7.) by phone the next work day.

16 **Look at the customer's questions. Write short answers.**

A: Hernan's Garage. Can I help you?

B: Yes, please. I want to drop off my car for a repair, but I have to work late. Do you have a night drop-off?

A: ________________________ (1.)

B: Great. Do I have to leave my car key in my car?

A: ________________________ (2.)

B: Can I get an estimate for the repair?

A: ________________________ (3.)

B: OK. I'll drop it off tonight. Thanks.

Name ______________________ ID ______________ Date ______________

UNIT 4

Your customers

➤ Vocabulary

1 **Read the sentences. What does each person need? Match each sentence with an item. Write the letter on the line.**

_____	**1.** She has a headache.	**a.** tissues
_____	**2.** My hair is dirty.	**b.** a thermometer
_____	**3.** He has a cold.	**c.** soap
_____	**4.** I'm going to brush my teeth.	**d.** a painkiller
_____	**5.** I want to wash my hands.	**e.** a hair dryer
_____	**6.** I think my child has a fever.	**f.** shampoo
_____	**7.** I just washed my hair.	**g.** toothpaste

2 **Complete the chart. Use personal care products and medicines from your book or use your own ideas.**

Things I use every day	Things I sometimes use

➤ Practical conversations

3 **Complete the conversations. Use words from the box.**

brand	store	ring it up	cough medicine	cheaper

1. **A:** Excuse me. I'd like to buy some ____________(1.).

   B: OK. Which ____________(2.) do you want?

   A: I'm not sure. Is the ____________(3.) brand good?

   B: Yes, it is. And it's ____________(4.). It's only $2.99.

   A: OK. I'll take it. Can you ____________(5.)?

   B: No, I'm sorry. The cashier can help you.

4 **Complete the conversations. Use the pictures or your <u>own</u> words.**

1. **A:** Is this ____________________ on sale?

   B: Which one?

   A: The ____________________.

   B: Yes, it is.

   A: What's the sale price?

   B: ____________________.

2. **A:** I'd like to get a rain check, please.

   B: OK. What did you want to buy?

   A: ____________________. But you're sold out.

   B: I'm sorry. Here you go. It's good for ____________________.

   A: Thanks.

Name ______________________ ID ____________ Date ____________

➤ Practical grammar

5 Complete each sentence with the comparative form of the adjective.

1. The weather here is ___colder___ (cold) than the weather in my country.
2. The park in your neighborhood is ________________ (beautiful) than the park in my neighborhood.
3. Store brand prices aren't always ________________ (cheap) than big brand prices.
4. Apartments in Old Town are ________________ (expensive) than houses in the city.
5. My car is________________ (old) than my son's car.
6. Subway stations in New York are ________________ (dirty) than stations in Boston.
7. This new camera is ________________ (bad) than my old camera!

6 ➤ CHALLENGE Write comparisons. Use the adjective.

1. Soft Touch tissues are $1.29. Quickway tissues are $.99. (cheap)

   Quickway tissues are cheaper than Soft Touch tissues.

2. Nice Smile toothpaste is good. Tooth-Right toothpaste isn't good. (good)

   ____

3. My bus is at 7:45 a.m. Your bus is at 8:00 a.m. (early)

   ____

4. Bell Food Store is cheap. Gourmet Deluxe Foods isn't cheap. (expensive)

   ____

5. Julio's apartment is dirty. Marcia's apartment isn't dirty. (clean)

   ____

6. This bottle has 100 aspirin tablets. That bottle has 250 aspirin tablets. (large)

   ____

7. This cashier is busy. That cashier isn't busy. (busy)

   ____

7 **Match each sentence on the left with a response on the right. Write the letter on the line.**

_____	**1.** I'd like a rain check for a camera.	**a.** The store one.
_____	**2.** Which shoes do you want to buy?	**b.** Which ones?
_____	**3.** Which apartment did you like?	**c.** The left one.
_____	**4.** Painkillers are on sale this week.	**d.** Which one?
_____	**5.** Which brand is usually cheaper?	**e.** The larger one.
_____	**6.** Which turn signal isn't working?	**f.** The red and black ones.

8 **Write the names of two supermarkets or drugstores you know. Write one name in each box.**

Compare the two stores. Answer the questions with complete sentences. Use your own words.

1. Which store is closer to your house or apartment?

____

2. Which store is cheaper?

____

3. Which one is cleaner?

____

4. Which one has better sale prices?

____

5. Where do you usually shop? Why?

____

Name ______________________ ID ____________ Date ____________

➤ Authentic practice

9 **Read. Choose your response. Circle the letter.**

1. "This VCR isn't what I wanted. I'd like to exchange it."

   a. OK. We have a better one on sale. **b.** OK. It's only $99.99.

2. "The cheaper ones are in the front, near the cash registers."

   a. Do you have any cheaper ones? **b.** Thank you.

3. "I'm sorry. We're sold out of that model."

   a. OK. Can I get a rain check? **b.** Terrific. I'll take one.

4. "There's something wrong with this camera."

   a. Oh, that's too bad. **b.** I'm looking for it.

5. "How long is it good for?"

   a. $2.00. **b.** Two months.

10 **Complete the conversation. Choose the correct response. Write the letter on the line.**

A: Did you call me, Esther?

B: ________ 1.

A: What's wrong?

B: ________ 2.

A: OK. What's the brand?

B: ________ 3.

A: OK. Fill in the brand and price on the form.

B: ________ 4.

A: Yes. Ask the customer to fill in her name and address.

B: ________ 5.

A: Give the customer one copy, and put the other copy in the box.

B: ________ 6.

a. OK. Anything else?
b. Yes, I did. Can you help me, please?
c. Smell Good. It's on sale for $1.99.
d. Great! Thanks a lot for your help.
e. I will. Now, what do I do with the form?
f. We're out of deodorant at the sale price, and this customer would like a rain check.

11 ➤ *CHALLENGE* **Look at the rain check. Then complete the paragraph.**

FAST LANE ELECTRONICS — RAIN CHECK

Item:	digital camera	Customer's Name:	Octavio Perez
Brand name and model:	Kodiak XS 1900	Customer's Address:	306 E. Pine St. Baltimore, MD 21213
Color:	black		
Sale price:	$299.99	Customer's phone number:	(410) 555-8719
Good until:	9/1	Date:	7/1

Do you want us to call you when your item comes in? ☑ yes ☐ no

On July 1, Mr. ________ (1.) went to Fast Lane Electronics. He wanted to buy a ________ (2.). The ________ (3.) brand camera, model number ________ (4.), was on sale for only ________ (5.). They had green ones, but he wanted a ________ (6.) one. He filled out a rain check. The store will ________ (7.) him when the camera comes in.

12 **Look at the rain check and the paragraph in Exercise 11 again. Then answer the questions.**

1. How long is the rain check good for? ________
2. Which color is sold out? ________
3. Which color is not sold out? ________

Name ______________________ ID ____________ Date ____________

13 **Read the conversation. Then fill in the rain check form. Use your <u>own</u> information and today's date.**

YOU Excuse me. I'm looking for a CD player.

Salesperson: OK. Which one did you want? We have a nice one on sale for $49.99.

YOU Actually I need something a little cheaper. The Music Master T-140 is in your sale ad for $19.99. That's the one I'd like to see.

Salesperson: I'm sorry. We sold the last one an hour ago.

YOU Oh no! I really wanted that one.

Salesperson: I'm sorry. Would you like a rain check for one?

YOU Yes, I guess so. Thanks.

Salesperson: Which color did you want?

YOU I like the blue one.

Salesperson: OK. Just fill in your personal information.

YOU Can you call me when it comes in?

Salesperson: Sure. Write your phone number on the form and we'd be happy to.

YOU Thanks.

FAST LANE ELECTRONICS

RAIN CHECK

Item: ______________	Customer's Name: ______________
Brand name and model: ______________	Customer's Address: ______________
Color: ______________	______________
Sale price: ______________	Customer's phone number: ______________
Good until: ______________	Date: ______________

Do you want us to call you when your item comes in? ❑ yes ❑ no

14 **Read the ad. Then complete the sentences. Circle the correct information.**

1. The toothbrushes are on sale for (one day / one week).
2. Discount Mart batteries are (cheaper / more expensive) than Energetic batteries.
3. The cameras are on sale for (one day / one week).
4. One bar of Blue Stripe soap on sale costs (50¢ / $1.00).
5. One bar of Discount Mart soap costs (40¢ / $4.00).

15 **Look at the ad in Exercise 14 again. Then write a sentence comparing the price of the two items.**

1. Discount Mart soap / Blue Stripe soap

   Discount Mart soap is cheaper than Blue Stripe soap.

2. color film / black and white film

   ____

3. store brand aspirin / Mayer aspirin

   ____

Name ______________________ ID ______________ Date ______________

UNIT 5

Your time

➤ Vocabulary

1 Complete the sentences. Write the missing letters on the line.

1. There's no bus on Sunday. Let's take the t__ ___ ___ ___ n__.
2. Do you want to buy a one-way t__ ___ ___ ___ ___ t__?
3. Hurry! The bus is l__ ___ ___ ___ i__ n__ g__ soon.
4. I'm late! It's a q__ ___ ___ ___ ___ ___ r__ to!
5. I want to arrive before 6:00. Let's take the e__ x__ ___ ___ ___ ___ s__.
6. What's the r__ ___ ___ ___ d__ - t__ r__ i__ p__ fare?
7. A f__ ___ ___ e__ c__ ___ ___ d__ is good for one week.

2 Look at the clocks. Match each clock with a time. Write the letter on the line.

a.

b.

c.

d.

e.

f.

_____ 1. a quarter after

_____ 2. ten forty

_____ 3. half past

_____ 4. a quarter to ten

_____ 5. twenty past

_____ 6. a quarter to eleven

3 Complete the sentences. Use words from the box.

missed the bus	stuck in traffic	had a flat tire	ran out of gas

1. I ____________________. I had to replace it.
2. I was one minute late, and I ____________________.
3. The gas warning light went on yesterday. I didn't go to the gas station and I ____________________ this morning.
4. The streets were very busy, and we were ____________________.

➤ Practical conversations

4 **Put the conversation in order. Write the number on the line.**

__1__ Can I still make the 6:45 train to Bridgeport?

_____ Can I take a bus to Bridgeport?

_____ Oh no! When did it leave?

_____ It's $2.30. Or you could buy a fare card.

_____ Yes. There's an express bus every thirty minutes. The next one's at 7:00. You'll be in Bridgeport before 7:30.

_____ Great. What's the fare?

_____ I'm sorry. You just missed it.

_____ One way. I'll take the train home.

_____ About two minutes ago.

_____ For a one-way or a round-trip ticket?

__11__ Great. Thanks.

5 **Complete the conversations. Use the schedules and your <u>own</u> words and times.**

1. **A:** I'd like a ticket to __________, please.
   B: Round trip or one way?
   A: __________.
   B: Here you go. That's $ __________, please.
   A: Thanks. Can I still make the __________?
   B: __________.

FROM HOVER PLAINS TO ROLLING HILLS

FARE	ONE-WAY	ROUND-TRIP
Hover Plains – Tuckdale	$3.25	$5.85
Hover Plains – Rolling Hills	$4.10	$7.40

LEAVE HOVER PLAINS	ARRIVE TUCKDALE	ARRIVE ROLLING HILLS
6:09	6:23	6:39
6:24	6:38	6:54
6:39	6:53	7:09

2. **A:** When's the next __________ to Centerville?
   B: Local or express?
   A: __________.
   B: They leave every __________.
   The next one leaves at __________.
   A: What's the fare?
   B: __________.

FROM WESTFIELD TO CENTERVILLE

Local Fare: $4.35 **Express Fare: $5.15**
x = Express

	LEAVE	ARRIVE
	8:15	9:10
x	8:20	9:00
	8:30	9:25
	8:45	9:40
x	8:50	9:30
	9:00	9:55
x	9:20	10:00

Name ______________________ ID ____________ Date ____________

➤ Practical grammar

6 **Complete each sentence with a form of <u>should</u> and the verb.**

1. The next train leaves in three minutes. You _should hurry_ (hurry).
2. We ______________ (not take) a taxi. It's too expensive.
3. The local bus arrives too late. You ______________ (take) the express.
4. You ______________ (go) now. You'll miss the bus!
5. You ______________ (not use) those eggs. They're too old.
6. We ______________ (buy) fare cards. They're cheaper than tokens.

7 **Look at the pictures. What should he or she do? Write your answers on the line. Use <u>should</u>.**

1.

2.

3.

1. ______________________________
2. ______________________________
3. ______________________________

8 **Complete the sentences. Write the letter on the line.**

1. The subway doesn't go to White Oak, but ______.
2. The local already left, but ______.
3. We could take a taxi, but ______.
4. I could drive, but ______.
5. A round-trip ticket is $3.40, but ______.
6. There's a new book store across the street. ______.

a. I don't want to be stuck in traffic
b. you could buy a fare card
c. We could go after work
d. you could take a bus
e. you could take the express
f. I don't see one

9 **Answer the questions with could. Use your own words.**

1. Your car won't start. What could you do?

____

2. You don't have to go to work tomorrow. What could you do?

____

3. You want to go to a restaurant for dinner tonight. Where could you go?

____

10 **Complete the sentences. Use could, couldn't, should, or shouldn't.**

1. You _____________ hurry! You _____________ still make the 7:30!
2. You _____________ take the local bus, but you'll be late.
3. I'm going to miss my bus! What _____________ I do?
4. The train doesn't go to Allentown, but you _____________ take a bus.
5. I had two flat tires this week! We _____________ buy new tires.
6. _____________ I take the subway? No, you _____________. It doesn't stop there.
7. The traffic is worse on Friday. You _____________ get stuck in traffic. You _____________ drive.

Name ______________________ ID ____________ Date ____________

➤ Authentic practice

11 Read. Choose your response. Circle the letter.

1. "The train is supposed to leave at 5:07."

   a. Can we still make it? **b.** Round trip or one way?

2. "You can either buy a token or get a fare card."

   a. No, I already have one. **b.** I'd like to buy a token, please.

3. "Haile called to say that he's stuck in traffic."

   a. He should take an earlier one. **b.** Is he going to be late?

4. "The train's going to leave at twenty to, and it's already 8:30!"

   a. Yes. In 10 minutes. **b.** We should hurry.

5. "I'm afraid you just missed the bus."

   a. Oh, no! **b.** That's good.

12 Read the conversation. Then look at the sentences. Check ☑ true or false.

Yen: Were you late this morning?

Julio: Yes, I was. I missed the bus. I had to take a later one.

Yen: Again? You just bought a car. Why are you still taking the bus?

Julio: Well, when I was driving home yesterday, I had a flat tire.

Yen: Couldn't you fix it?

Julio: I fixed it! I fixed it last night.

Yen: So then why were you taking the bus this morning?

Julio: Because after I fixed the tire, I drove to my mother's house, and I ran out of gas!

	true	false
1. Julio drove his new car yesterday.	❑	❑
2. Julio didn't drive to work today because he had a flat tire.	❑	❑
3. Yen fixed the flat tire.	❑	❑
4. Julio had the flat tire before he ran out of gas.	❑	❑
5. Julio took the bus today.	❑	❑

13 Look at the schedule. Then complete the sentences. Use words from the box.

Front Street bus schedule

Weekday mornings (inbound)
Express buses are in **bold** type.

Gateway Mall	20th St.	30th St.	40th St.	Central Station
6:05	6:23	6:35	6:50	6:55
6:35	6:53	7:05	7:20	7:25
7:00	------	**7:20**	------	**7:30**
7:05	7:23	7:35	7:50	7:55
7:35	7:53	8:05	8:20	8:25
8:00	------	**8:20**	------	**8:30**

before	hurry	stop	6:55	later	7:55	after

1. There's an express bus at 7:00. The next express leaves an hour ________.
2. You could take the 7:35 from Gateway Mall, but you'll arrive at Central Station ________ 8:00.
3. The express buses don't ________ at 20th Street.
4. Three buses stop at 30th Street ________ 7:30.
5. The first bus in the morning arrives at Central Station at ________.
6. I took the 7:23 from the 20th Street stop. It was five minutes late, so I arrived at the 40th Street stop at ________.
7. You should arrive at the stop five or ten minutes before the bus leaves. Then you won't have to ________.

14 Look at the bus schedule in Exercise 13 again. Then answer the questions.

1. What time does the 7:35 from Gateway Mall arrive at the 40th Street stop?

____

2. I just missed the 7:00 express. What time does the next express leave?

____

3. Do the local buses leave every twenty minutes from Gateway Mall in the morning?

____

4. You're at 20th Street at 7:00. You need to arrive at Central Station before 8:00. Which bus could you take?

____

Name ______________________ ID ____________ Date ____________

15 **Read the sentences. Then complete the bus schedule. Write in every box.**

Front Street line bus

Weekday afternoon (Outbound)

Express buses are in **bold** type.

Central Station	40th St.	30th St.	20th St.	Gateway Mall
4:03	4:08	4:23	4:35	
4:30	------	**4:40**	------	**5:00**
4:33		4:53	5:05	5:23
	5:08	5:23	5:35	
5:30				**6:00**

1. You can take a bus at 30th Street at 4:23. It arrives at Gateway Mall thirty minutes later.
2. In the afternoon, a local bus leaves from 40th Street every thirty minutes.
3. The first bus after 5:00 leaves Central Station at 5:03. It gets to Gateway Mall at 5:53.
4. The 5:30 express stops at 30th Street at 5:40. It doesn't stop at 40th Street or at 20th Street.

16 **Look at the sign. Then complete the sentences.**

Rush hour fares are in effect at high traffic times Monday through Friday. (See the schedule below.)				
before 6 a.m. standard $0.90	6 a.m. –9 a.m. rush $1.20	9 a.m.–3 p.m. standard $0.90	3 p.m.–7 p.m. rush $1.20	after 7 p.m. standard $0.90
There are no rush hour fares on weekends and holidays. Standard fares are in effect all day Saturday and Sunday.				

1. On Tuesday at 7:30 a.m., the fare is $ __________.
2. On Thursday at 8:00 p.m., the fare is $ __________.
3. At 5:45 a.m. on Tuesday, the fare is $ __________.
4. At 3:30 p.m. on Friday, the fare is $ __________.
5. On Saturday at 12:00 noon, the fare is $ __________.

17 **Look at Petra's e-mail. Check ☑ yes or no.**

From: Petra Mishkoff
CC:
To: Jenny Davies

Subject: Travel tomorrow

Message:

Hi, Jenny,

I wanted to ask you about how to get to the meeting tomorrow. Is it better to drive or to take the train? I'd like to take the train because I don't want to be stuck in traffic. I don't want to be late. If I take the train, I'll leave from Highland Station. Should I take the 7:30 or the 8:00? And which station should I go to—Abbott Street or Sixth Street? Thanks for your help!

—Petra

	yes	no
1. Petra needs to go to a meeting tomorrow.	☐	☐
2. Petra wants to drive to the meeting.	☐	☐
3. Petra's train leaves from Abbott Street in the morning.	☐	☐
4. Petra can take a train at 7:30 a.m. or 8:00 a.m.	☐	☐

18 ➤ ***CHALLENGE*** **Petra needs directions to the meeting. She asked Jenny to send the directions in an e-mail. Look at Jenny's words. Then complete Jenny's e-mail message to Petra.**

"Petra should take the train. It's better than driving, and faster. She should take the 7:30 from Highland Station. The 8:00 arrives after 9:00, and that's too late. She could take the train to the Abbott Street station or the Sixth Street station, but the Sixth Street station is better."

From: Jenny Davies
CC:
To: Petra Mishkoff

Subject: Re: Travel tomorrow

Message:

Hi, Petra,

You shouldn't __________ (1.). You __________ (2.) take the train. From Highland Station, you should take the __________ (3.) train because the 8:00 __________ (4.) __________ (5.) 9:00. You should go to the __________ (6.) station. See you tomorrow.

—Jenny

Name ______________________ ID ____________ Date ____________

UNIT 6

Your supplies and resources

➤ Vocabulary

1 Complete the sentences. Use words from the box.

rubber gloves	change	bathtub	beds
blanket	vacuum cleaner	pillow	cleanser

1. The bathtub is really dirty. You'll need a sponge and a good ______________.
2. Ms. Teixeira is a hotel housekeeper. She cleans rooms and makes ______________.
3. I have a problem with this bed. The ______________ is larger than the pillowcase.
4. We're going to wash the van. Should we wear ______________?
5. The ______________ isn't working. How are we going to clean these rooms?
6. Please vacuum the room before you ______________ the sheets.
7. It's going to snow tonight! Do you want a warmer ______________?
8. The bathroom has a ______________ and a shower.

2 Complete the chart. List products and items you have in your house or apartment. Use items from your book or use your <u>own</u> words.

In my closet	In my bathroom	In my bedroom
towels	a shower	a bed

➤ Practical conversations

3 **Complete the conversation. Choose the correct response. Write the letter on the line.**

A: I'm going to the supply room. Do you need anything?

B: ________ 1.

A: Sure. I'll pick them up. Anything else?

B: ________ 2.

A: OK. I'll get it. Do you need any cleanser?

B: ________ 3.

A: Would you like me to empty the trash before I go?

B: ________ 4.

A: OK. Let me know if you need anything else.

B: ________ 5.

a. Oh, thanks for offering, but I can empty it.

b. Thanks. I really appreciate it.

c. Actually, I do. Could you get me some paper towels?

d. Well, I could use a new bottle of furniture polish.

e. No, thanks. That's all.

4 **Complete the conversations. Use your own words.**

1. A: Do you need anything from the supply cart?

   B: Yes, please. Could you get me a ______________________________?

   A: Sure. Anything else?

   B: Actually, you could get me some ______________________________ too.

   A: ______________________________. I'll be right back.

   B: ______________________________.

2. A: Are you going to the supply closet?

   B: Yes, I am. Would you like me to get you anything?

   A: ____.

   B: ______________________________.

Name ______________________ ID ____________ Date ____________

➤ Practical grammar

5 **Make two sentences. Use too or either.**

1. I need some trash bags and Maia needs some trash bags.
   I need some trash bags. Maia does too.
2. The bedroom is clean and the bathroom is clean.
   ____
3. The toilet isn't working and the sink isn't working.
   ____
4. Joan works on the 9th floor and Asha works on the 9th floor.
   ____
5. Toilet paper is on sale and paper towels are on sale.
   ____
6. These blankets aren't expensive and these sheets aren't expensive.
   ____
7. The housekeepers don't do the laundry and the managers don't do the laundry.
   ____

6 **Look at the pictures. Write a, an, or the on the line.**

1.

2.

3.

4.

7 **Complete the sentences. Write a, an, or the on the line.**

1. I need to clean my bathroom. ______________ bathtub is really dirty.
2. I'm going to make my bed. I need two clean sheets and ______________ clean pillowcase.
3. There are two washcloths on the shelf. One is red and one is blue. Could you give me ______________ blue one, please?
4. I'm going to buy some toothpaste and ______________ new toothbrush.
5. I'll need to look at the engine. Could you please open ______________ hood?
6. Rubio has ______________ old truck. He wants to buy ______________ new one.
7. You missed the 3:15 train, but you could take ______________ 3:35.

8 **➤CHALLENGE** **Look at the answers. Complete the questions. Use the present continuous.**

1. When are you buying a new vacuum cleaner ______________?
   I'm buying a new vacuum cleaner on Saturday.
2. Why ____?
   I'm buying a new vacuum cleaner because the old one isn't working.
3. Where ____?
   I'm buying it at Appliance Land.
4. Who ____?
   Anabel is helping me look at vacuum cleaners.
5. What ____?
   I'm cleaning my house after I buy the vacuum cleaner.

9 **Complete the sentences about yourself. Use the present continuous.**

1. On Saturday, ____.
2. Next week, my friends and I ____.
3. ____ tomorrow night.

Name ______________________ ID ______________ Date ______________

➤ Authentic practice

10 **Read. Choose <u>your</u> response. Circle the letter.**

1. "Let me know if there's anything you'd like me to do."

   a. Thanks. I do. b. OK. I appreciate it.

2. "Would you like me to help you with that?"

   a. Thanks for offering, but I can do it. b. Actually, I do too.

3. "I'm going to the supermarket. Can I get you anything while I'm there?"

   a. I'll be right back. b. Sure, you could get me some paper towels.

4. "I'm practically out of vacuum cleaner bags."

   a. Actually, I am too. b. Actually, I'm not either.

5. "Thanks for helping me out. I really appreciate it."

   a. I'd be glad to. b. Anytime.

11 **Complete the conversations. Use words from the box.**

appreciate	change	offering	glad	right	empty

1. **A:** You're working late today. Would you like some help?

   B: Yes, I would. I really ______________ it.

2. **A:** Would you be nice enough to get us some paper from the office closet?

   B: Sure. No problem. I'll be ______________ back.

3. **A:** Could you please vacuum the hallway carpet? I'm really busy.

   B: Sure. I'd be ______________ to.

4. **A:** Would you like me to ______________ the trash? It's 5:00.

   B: That would be great, thanks. And thanks for ______________.

5. **A:** Could you give me a hand? I want to ______________ the oil in my car, and I need help.

   B: I'd be happy to help. I'll be right there.

12 **Monique and Pierre Leffler have two children, Anje and Luc. At their house, everyone helps with the housework. Monique made a chart of the family's jobs. Look at the job chart. Then check ☑ yes or no.**

	Make your own bed	Clean the bathroom	Vacuum the living room	Wash the dishes after dinner	Do the laundry	Take out the trash and recycling
Mon	Monique, Anje, Luc			Anje		Anje
Tue	Monique, Anje, Luc	Anje	Luc	Luc		
Wed	Monique, Anje, Luc			Anje	Monique	
Thu	Monique, Anje, Luc			Luc		Luc
Fri	Monique, Anje, Luc	Luc	Anje	Pierre		
Sat	Monique, Anje, Luc			Anje		
Sun	Monique, Anje, Luc			Luc	Pierre	

	yes	no
1. Monique doesn't make her bed every day.	❑	❑
2. Anje doesn't do the laundry. Luc doesn't either.	❑	❑
3. Pierre washes the dishes after dinner on Thursday.	❑	❑
4. Monique does the laundry once a week.	❑	❑
5. Today is Tuesday. Luc is taking out the trash tomorrow.	❑	❑
6. Anje cleans the bathroom once a week. Pierre does too.	❑	❑

Name ______________________ ID ______________ Date ______________

13 **Read the sign.**

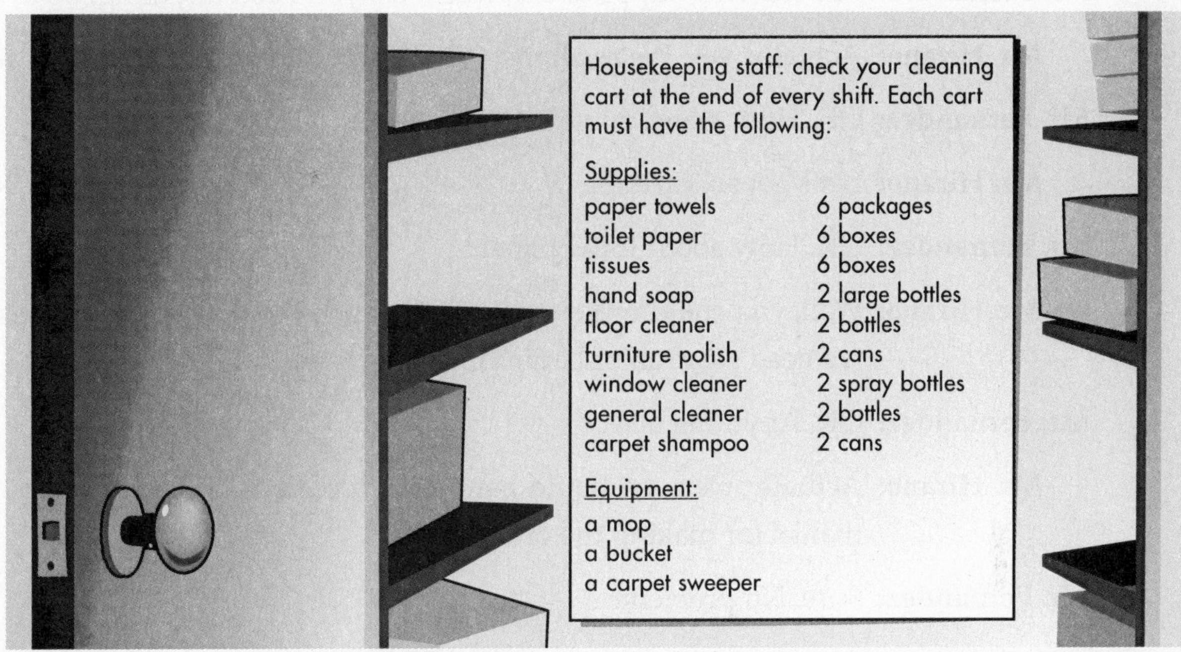

Housekeeping staff: check your cleaning cart at the end of every shift. Each cart must have the following:
Supplies:
paper towels 6 packages
toilet paper 6 boxes
tissues 6 boxes
hand soap 2 large bottles
floor cleaner 2 bottles
furniture polish 2 cans
window cleaner 2 spray bottles
general cleaner 2 bottles
carpet shampoo 2 cans
Equipment:
a mop
a bucket
a carpet sweeper

Alicia Rosario is a housekeeper on the first floor of the Redwood Hotel and Conference Center. She just finished her shift, and she is checking her cleaning cart. Look at her cleaning cart. What supplies does she need?

1. __5__ paper towels
2. ______ toilet paper
3. ______ tissues
4. ______ hand soap
5. ______ floor cleaner
6. ______ furniture polish
7. ______ window cleaner
8. ______ general cleaner
9. ______ carpet shampoo
10. ______ mop
11. ______ bucket
12. ______ carpet sweeper

14 **Oshi Hirano and Saul Fernandez work for the Eastland School District. Read their conversation. Then complete the order form for Mr. Fernandez.**

Mr. Fernandez: I'm ordering supplies this week. Do you need anything?

Mr. Hirano: Actually, yes. We're almost out of paper towels in the supply room.

Mr. Fernandez: OK. How many do you need?

Mr. Hirano: Let's get six cartons.

Mr. Fernandez: OK. How about toilet paper?

Mr. Hirano: Well, you could order some toilet paper. We need three cartons. And we need a carton of bathroom cleaner too.

Mr. Fernandez: OK. Anything else?

Mr. Hirano: Actually, we need liquid hand soap too. Let's order six bottles. And thanks for making the order.

Mr. Fernandez: Sure. No problem.

R-400 Requisition Form

Eastland School District

To order supplies, fill out this form completely and send it to the Central Supplies Office in Hanover.

Today's date: ______________________

Item	Quantity

Item	Quantity

15 *CHALLENGE* **Saul Fernandez is writing a note to his co-worker Jorge Samadi. He wants to tell Jorge when he is ordering supplies. He also offers to order supplies for Jorge. Complete Saul's note.**

Hi Jorge,

____

____

____

Saul

Name ______________________ ID ______________ Date ______________

UNIT 7

Your relationships

➤ Vocabulary

1 Complete the sentences. Write the letter on the line.

1. Mrs. Lee has her own small book store; she's a _____.
2. I had an interview at Choi's Garage, but I didn't _____.
3. Rosa and Elisa opened a cleaning company; they're _____.
4. Malika got a promotion; now she's a _____.
5. My sister rented the apartment next door; she's going to be my _____.
6. Jack was late every day and he never called the supervisor; that's why he _____.
7. The manager at the new Super 7 called me today; I _____!
8. Leo and I are cashiers at Pizza Palace; we're _____.

a. supervisor
b. got fired
c. neighbor
d. get hired
e. partners
f. co-workers
g. store owner
h. got hired

2 Complete the sentences.

1. My husband's brother is my *brother-in-law*.
2. My mother and my father are my ____________________.
3. My daughter's husband is my ____________________.
4. My mother's father and my mother's mother are my ____________________.
5. My wife's mother is my ____________________.
6. My daughter and my son are my ____________________.

➤ Practical conversations

3 Complete the conversations. Use words from the box.

Really	better	against the rules	get along
disagree	work it out	discuss	check with

1. **A:** Is smoking inside ________________________?
   1.

   B: I think so, but I'm not sure.

   A: Who can I ________________________?
   2.

   B: You'd ________________________ ask the office manager.
   3.

   A: OK. Thanks.

2. **A:** How do you ________________________ with your husband's parents?
   4.

   B: I like them. But sometimes we ________________________ about the children.
   5.

   A: Can you ________________________ it with them?
   6.

   B: Yes, I can. And usually we can ________________________.
   7.

   A: ________________________? That's good.
   8.

4 Complete the conversations. Use your own words.

1. **A:** Do you get along with ________________________?

   B: Well, we usually get along. But we disagree about ________________________.

   A: If you discuss ________________________ with ________________________, maybe you can work it out.

   B: It's worth a try.

2. **A:** Can we ________________________ at work?

   B: I'm not sure. You'd better check with ________________________.

   A: OK, I will. Thanks for ________________________.

Name ______________________ ID ____________ Date ____________

➤ Practical grammar

5 ➤ **CHALLENGE** **Put the words in order. Write sentences. Begin each sentence with If.**

1. ~~If~~ / ~~it~~ / , / the bathroom / dirty / clean / please / is

   If ______________________________ it.

2. ~~If~~ / get / , / call / I / ~~my parents~~ / the job / I'll

   If ______________________________ my parents.

3. ~~If~~ / the car / run out of / will / you / don't / , / you / fill up / ~~gas~~

   If ______________________________ gas.

4. ~~If~~ / won't need / you / have / , / ~~a ticket~~ / a / fare card / you

   If ______________________________ a ticket.

5. ~~If~~ / give / I'll / you're not / to / at home / , / it / ~~your neighbor~~

   If ______________________________ your neighbor.

6. ~~If~~ / please / you / get / go to / some / me / the drugstore / , / ~~toothpaste~~

   If ______________________________ toothpaste.

6 **Complete the sentences. Use your own words.**

1. If ______________________________, you'll get fired.
2. If ______________________________, call me.
3. If ______________________________, maybe you'll get a promotion.
4. If ______________________________, you should discuss it with me.

7 **Complete the conversations. Use had better or 'd better and your own words.**

1. **A:** It's going to snow tomorrow.

   B: We ______________________________.

2. **A:** We can't park on the street. It's against the rules.

   B: We ______________________________.

3. **A:** I want to offer you a promotion, but you'll have to work the night shift.

   B: I ______________________________.

8 **Complete the sentences. Use better or rather.**

1. I don't like to work from 9 to 5. I'd ______________ go home earlier.
2. You'd ______________ check with the owner. I don't know the answer.
3. If you need to know soon, you'd ______________ call the office now.
4. Where would you ______________ go—to the coffee shop or to the bookstore?
5. We'd ______________ not take the local bus. It's already late, and we really have to arrive on time.

9 **➤CHALLENGE** **Compare the two choices. Write which choice you like better. Write your reason.**

1. the early shift — the late shift

   I'd rather work the early shift because I want to eat dinner with my family.

2. full-time — part-time

   ____

   ____

3. discuss a problem with my friends — discuss a problem with my relatives

   ____

   ____

4. an apartment — a house

   ____

   ____

5. a small drugstore — a big drugstore

   ____

   ____

Name ______________________ ID ____________ Date ____________

➤ Authentic practice

10 Read. Choose your response. Circle the letter.

1. "My neighbors aren't getting along."

   a. I'm sorry to hear that. **b.** It's worth a try.

2. "It might be against the rules to make a personal call."

   a. Really? **b.** Can I tell you next week?

3. "Thanks for listening to me talk about my problems."

   a. Tomorrow's fine. **b.** Anytime.

4. "Thanks for offering, but I'd rather work it out myself."

   a. Let me know if there's anything you need. **b.** I'd rather not.

5. "To tell you the truth, I don't think I can fix it."

   a. Thanks for telling me. **b.** OK, but I can't call you from work.

11 Read the conversation. Write the names on the lines.

A: I'd like to register my daughter, Sophie Valdez-Simms, for childcare.

B: All right. Let me fill out this form. I need your name and your wife's name.

A: My name is Gary Simms and my wife is Lucia Valdez.

B: OK, thanks. Now I need two names of people we can call if there's an emergency.

A: Well, you could call my brother-in-law. His name is Rafael Valdez. And my father-in-law is home all day, so you could call him. His name is Jose Valdez.

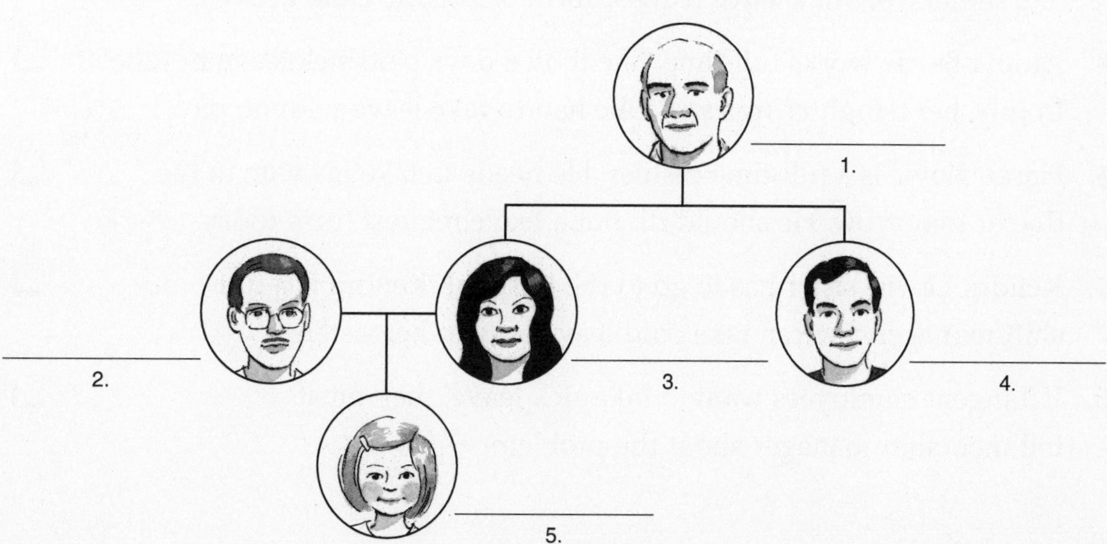

12 **Read the Tangent Department Store employee manual.**

TANGENT
Department Store

Benefits Policy

Sick leave and family benefits are available to full-time employees; you must fill out a leave request form and drop it off at the office.

Privacy Policy

You do not have to discuss personal information about yourself or your family with your manager.

Sick Leave Policy

Each employee is entitled to 6 days (48 hours) of paid sick leave a year. You may also take paid sick leave if a relative in your immediate family (child, husband, wife, parent, or parent-in-law only) is sick or injured, or must visit the doctor. If you take more than 6 days in one year, any day after 6 days will be without pay.

If you know in advance that you will need sick leave, please fill out a leave request form the day before you need sick leave.

Family Leave Policy

Employees are entitled to family leave with pay when a new child is born to the employee, adopted by the employee, or taken into the family by foster care. Employees are entitled to one month of family leave for each new child.

You must apply for family leave at least one month before the new child arrives. If you do not know the exact date you will need to begin family leave, you may discuss the possible dates with your shift manager. Put an approximate date on your leave request form.

Read about these Tangent employees. Then check ☑ true or false.

	true	false
1. Xu Wang works for Tangent part-time on the night shift. He can get sick leave benefits.	❑	❑
2. Angela de Soto is having a baby in August. She works full-time. She should fill out a leave request form before the child arrives.	❑	❑
3. Amina Barrie works full-time. She took 6 days paid sick leave in June. In July, her daughter was sick. She had to take leave with no pay.	❑	❑
4. Hasen Kovic is a full-time cashier. He needs to take his wife to the doctor tomorrow. He should fill out a leave request form today.	❑	❑
5. Kendra Lewis' sister has to go to the hospital. Kendra is a full-time shift manager. She can take paid leave to help her sister.	❑	❑
6. If Tangent employees want to take sick leave, they must tell their shift manager about the problem.	❑	❑

Name ______________________ ID ____________ Date ____________

13 **Look at Exercise 12 again. Fill out the leave request form for Hasen Kovic. Use tomorrow's date for the date of leave requested.**

TANGENT
Department Store

Leave Request Form

Employee's name ______________________________________
Last First

Employee's status: ☐ full-time ☐ part-time Position: ____________________

Today's date: ______/______/______
Month Day Year

Date of leave requested: ______/______/______
Month Day Year

If more than one day is requested, when will leave end? ______/______/______
Month Day Year

Type of leave (check one):

☐ Sick leave: employee

☐ Sick leave: immediate relative

☐ Family leave

14 **Anton Wu is a new employee at Tangent. Answer his questions about the leave policy.**

1. **Mr. Wu:** I'm a full-time employee. If I get sick, can I take paid sick leave?

   YOU ____.

2. **Mr. Wu:** How many days of paid sick leave can I take in a year?

   YOU ____.

3. **Mr. Wu:** After I fill out a leave request form, what should I do with it?

   YOU ____.

4. **Mr. Wu:** My wife and I are having a new baby in February. When should I fill out a leave request form?

   YOU ____.

5. **Mr. Wu:** Do I have to tell the manager why I want to take sick leave?

   YOU ____.

15 **Can you do these things at your workplace? Check ☑ yes or no.**

	yes	no
1. I can smoke at my workplace.	❑	❑
2. I can bring my children to work.	❑	❑
3. I can make a personal call.	❑	❑
4. I can listen to music when I'm working.	❑	❑
5. I can wear a T-shirt and jeans to work.	❑	❑
6. I can park in the parking lot.	❑	❑

16 ➤ ***CHALLENGE*** **Complete the conversations. Give advice. Use your own words.**

1. **A:** I think the manager and the owner disagree about smoking.

   B: Really?

   A: Yes. The owner told me it's against the rules if smoke inside, but I think the manager smokes in the building.

   B: Should we tell the owner?

   A: ______________________ because ______________________________

   ____.

2. **A:** My neighbor and her husband aren't getting along very well.

   B: I'm sorry to hear that.

   A: Me too. Do you think I should give them some advice?

   B: ______________________ because ______________________________

   ____.

Name ______________________ ID ______________ Date ______________

UNIT 8

Your health and safety

Vocabulary

1 Look at the pictures. Then complete the sentences.

1. You should check the ______________________ in your apartment twice a year.

2. If the fire is small, use a ______________________.

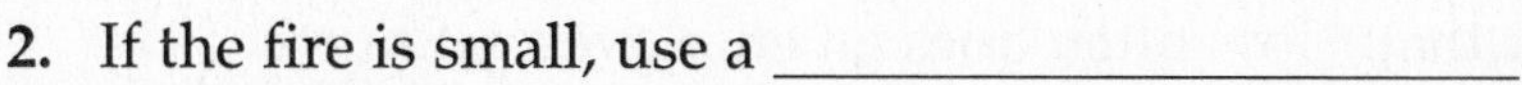

3. Don't ______________________! You should walk across the street at the corner.

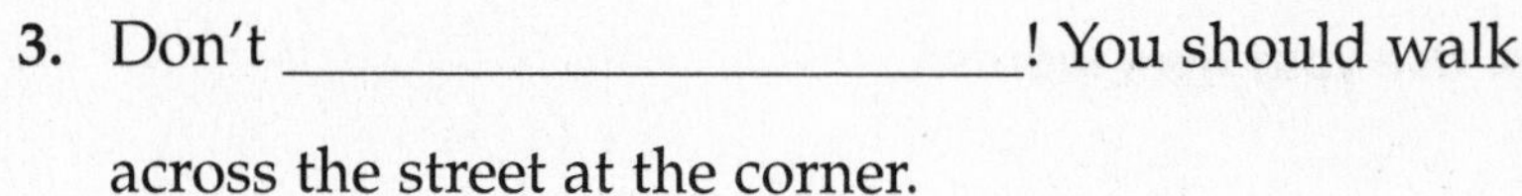

4. Don't do that! You'll get a ______________________.

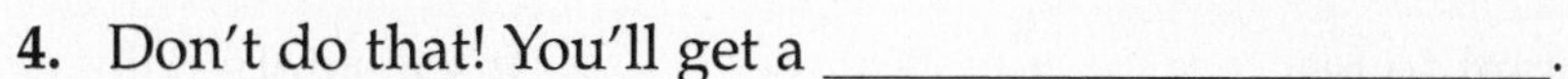

5. Don't jaywalk. You don't want to get ______________________.

6. There's some water on the floor. Be careful! Don't ______________________.

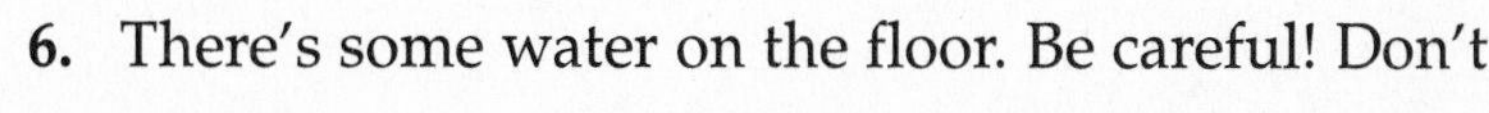

2 Complete the sentences. Follow the example. Use your own words.

1. I eat rice twice a week.
2. I talk to ______________________
3. My friends and I ______________________
4. I buy ______________________
5. I clean ______________________

➤ Practical conversations

3 **Put the conversation in order. Write the number on the line.**

__1__ Is this job dangerous?

_____ OK. I'll be careful. Anything else?

_____ Yes. One more thing. Sometimes there's water on the floor. I slipped and fell once last year.

_____ Not often. You just have to be careful.

_____ Why? What's wrong?

_____ Well, the hot food is really hot, and you might get burned.

_____ No, it's not really dangerous. But we have to be careful in the kitchen.

_____ I'm sorry to hear that. How often does an employee get hurt?

__9__ OK. I will.

4 **Complete the conversations. Use your <u>own</u> words.**

1. **A:** Did you test the ______________________ this month?

   B: No, I didn't. Why?

   A: It's really important to test ______________________. It's a safety rule.

   B: You're right. How often should I test ______________________?

   A: ______________________ a ______________________.

   B: OK. I'd better do it now. Thanks.

2. **A:** Look out!

   B: Why? What's wrong?

   A: That ______________________ is ______________________. You might ______________________.

   B: Thanks for ______________________. I didn't see it.

   A: You're welcome.

Name ______________________ ID ____________ Date ____________

➤ Practical grammar

5 Look at the warning signs. Then complete the sentences. Use might.

1. Don't put the hair dryer in the sink. You ______________________________.

2. If you touch this, you ______________________________.

3. Don't drink this water. You ______________________________.

4. Be careful! Walking here is dangerous. You ______________________________.

5. Don't put this where your children can get it. They ______________________________.

6 Write sentences. Use words from each box.

You I We	might might not	run out of gas get hit by a car get fired get really sick miss class	if	you you don't I I don't we we don't	fill up the car now. take the express train. take this medicine every day. break the rules. jaywalk.

1. *You might run out of gas if you don't fill up the car now.*
2. ______________________________
3. ______________________________
4. ______________________________
5. ______________________________

7 **Complete each conversation with <u>I will</u> or <u>I won't</u>.**

1. A: If you'd like to work late this weekend, tell the shift manager.

   B: OK. ________________.

2. A: That drill is dangerous. Don't use it.

   B: All right. ________________.

3. A: You should never use a hair dryer near water. You could really get hurt.

   B: Thanks. ________________.

4. A: You need to read the warnings on this machine before you use it.

   B: ________________.

5. A: Smell that soup before you eat it. It's really old.

   B: ________________.

6. A: You can't take your friend with you to a job interview!

   B: Don't worry. ____________.

8 **Complete the sentences with <u>might</u>, <u>should</u>, <u>will</u>, or <u>won't</u>.**

1. I ____________ get a promotion at my job, but I'm not sure.
2. I ____________ wash my car tomorrow because I just washed it yesterday.
3. You're right. I really ____________ go to a doctor for my cold.
4. Don't worry. I'm sure your co-workers ____________ help you.

9 **➤CHALLENGE** **Complete the sentences about <u>yourself</u>. Use <u>might</u>, <u>should</u>, <u>will</u>, or <u>won't</u>.**

1. I ____________ get a promotion at my job because ____________________________

   ____.

2. I ____________ wash my hair tomorrow because ______________________________

   ____.

3. I ____________ check the safety equipment in my home because ______________

   ____.

4. My relatives ____________ discuss their problems with me because ____________

   ____.

Name ______________________ ID ______________ Date ______________

➤ Authentic practice

10 Read. Choose your response. Circle the letter.

1. "You've got to be careful with the hot pot."
   a. I don't know. **b.** Thanks. I won't forget.
2. "I think I smell gas. Why don't we check the stove?"
   a. Good idea. **b.** I don't see it.
3. "We're out of batteries. Don't forget to get some when you go out."
   a. Don't worry. I'll remember. **b.** Why? What's wrong?
4. "Could you check the sink in the men's restroom? I hear water running."
   a. It's important. Don't forget. **b.** Sure. I'll be right back.
5. "Make sure you're wearing rubber shoes when you use this equipment."
   a. OK. Thanks for warning me. **b.** OK. I won't.

11 Complete the conversation. Choose the correct response. Write the letter on the line.

A: I think there's a problem with the smoke detector.

B: ______ 1.

A: Well, I don't think it's working.

B: ______ 2.

A: No, I didn't. How do I test it?

B: ______ 3.

A: I'll try it. And how often should I change the battery?

B: ______ 4.

A: How do I remember?

B: ______ 5.

A: OK, I will. And thanks for telling me.

B: ______ 6.

a. Every 6 months.
b. Replace it when you change your clocks—in April and October.
c. Sure. It's important!
d. What's wrong?
e. That's dangerous. Did you test it?
f. Just push the small red button. If it's working, it will beep.

12 **Fill in the fire safety checklist for yourself. Then check your score.**

SAFETY FIRST!

How safe is your home? Fill out this fire safety checklist and find out!

	yes	no
1. Do you smoke in bed?	⬭	⬭
2. Do you have a lot of trash in your home?	⬭	⬭
3. Do you keep gasoline in your home?	⬭	⬭
4. Do you leave the kitchen when you are cooking on the stove?	⬭	⬭
5. Is there trash or dust under or behind your clothes dryer?	⬭	⬭
6. Are any smoke detectors older than 10 years old?	⬭	⬭
7. Do you have a fire extinguisher in your home or building?	⬭	⬭
8. Do you know how to use the fire extinguisher?	⬭	⬭
9. Do you keep matches where children can't get them?	⬭	⬭
10. Do you have a smoke detector outside every bedroom and on every floor of your home?	⬭	⬭
11. Do you test your smoke detectors every month?	⬭	⬭
12. Do you replace the batteries in your smoke detectors every 6 months?	⬭	⬭
13. Can emergency vehicles see your house number from the street?	⬭	⬭
14. Does your family know how to get out of the house if there is a fire?	⬭	⬭
15. Do you have emergency numbers posted near your telephone?	⬭	⬭

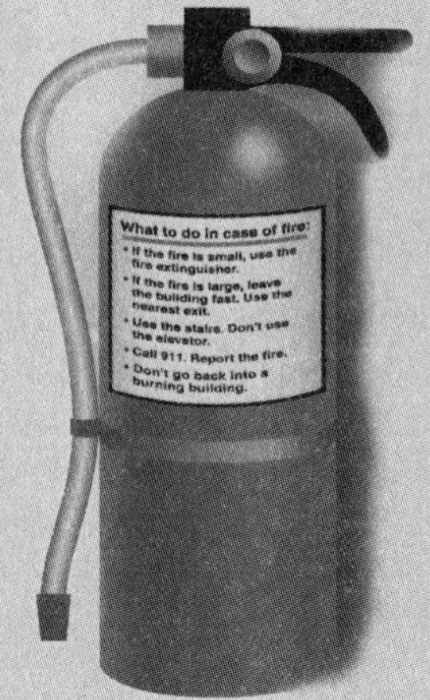

A. Look at questions 1–6. How many 'no' answers do you have? ______

B. Look at questions 7–15. How many 'yes' answers do you have? + ______

C. To get your score, add the total for lines A and B.

*If your answer is 0–11, look out! You need to start making your home safer right now!

*If your answer is 12–14, you should make a few changes. Do it now!

*If your answer is 15, congratulations! Keep up the good work!

Name ______________________ ID ____________ Date ____________

13 Read the safety information on the fire extinguisher.

Read all the warnings on this label and in the owner's manual before you use this fire extinguisher!

Safety Warnings:

- Keep this fire extinguisher out of children's reach.
- Do not burn the fire extinguisher.
- Do not discharge the extinguisher near a person's face.
- Do not store the extinguisher in very hot or very cold temperatures.
- Check the pressure gauge at the top of the extinguisher once a month.
- If the pressure is low, take the extinguisher to a service center for service.

Important:

- When you use this extinguisher on a fire, the fire might look larger at first. This is normal; the fire is not really larger. Do not stop spraying the fire.
- This fire extinguisher will spray for about 10 seconds.

Important:

This is an A B C fire extinguisher. It can be used on

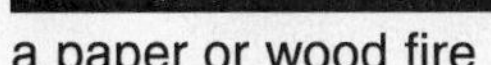

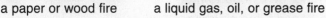

a paper or wood fire

a liquid gas, oil, or grease fire

an electrical fire

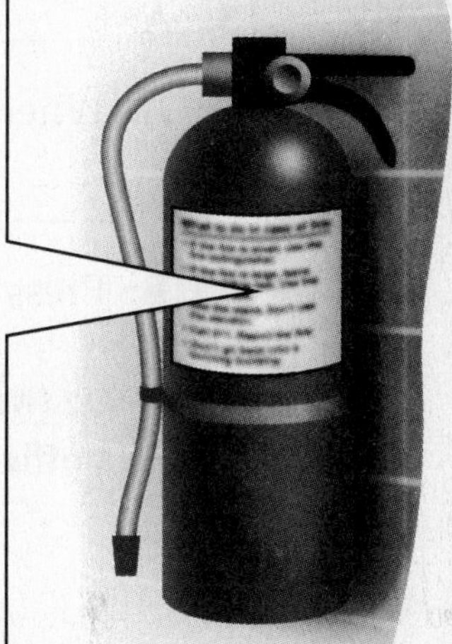

Read the sentences. Check ☑ true or false.

	true	false
1. It's OK to keep the fire extinguisher outside in very cold weather.	☐	☐
2. You should check the pressure gauge once a year.	☐	☐
3. This fire extinguisher can be used on a paper fire.	☐	☐
4. You can use this fire extinguisher for about 10 minutes.	☐	☐
5. You should read all the warnings before you use the fire extinguisher.	☐	☐

14 Read the label on the smoke detector. Look at the answers. Then complete the questions on page 64.

- Have at least one smoke detector on each floor of your home.
- Replace the battery when the smoke detector makes a beeping sound every 20 seconds.
- Use a 9-volt battery only.
- Test the battery once a month.
- To test the battery, press the red test button. If the detector is working, it will make a long beep.

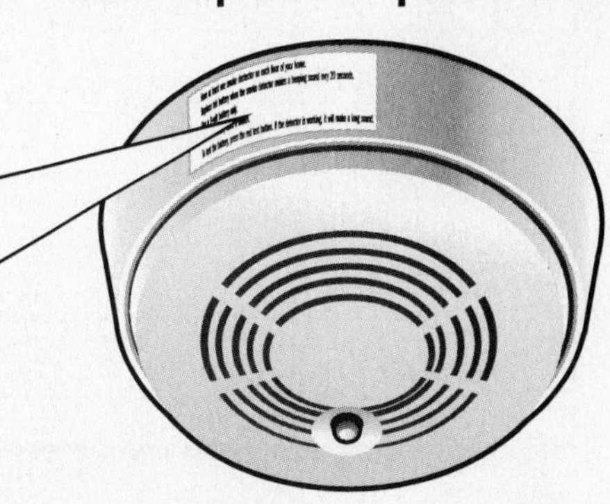

1. **A:** How many smoke detectors ______________________________?

   B: You should have at least one on each floor of your house.

2. **A:** ______________________________ test the battery?

   B: Once a month.

3. **A:** ______________________________ replace the battery?

   B: When the detector makes a short beeping sound.

4. **A:** ______________________________ test the battery?

   B: Press the red test button.

15 ➤ ***CHALLENGE*** **Isabel and Rhoda are co-workers at a child care center. Isabel called Rhoda's office and left this message on the answering machine. Read Isabel's message.**

"Hi, Rhoda. It's Isabel. Could you do me a favor? I have a doctor's appointment tomorrow before work, so I might be a little late. Could you write a note to Bui for me and explain that I might be late? Also, please warn him that if it rains tomorrow morning, he'll need to mop the front hall. If he doesn't, the children might slip and fall. Thanks."

Complete Rhoda's note to Bui.

Bui—

____

____

____

Thanks,

Rhoda

Name ______________________ ID ______________ Date ______________

UNIT 9

Your money

➤ Vocabulary

1 
Look at the pictures. Circle the letter.

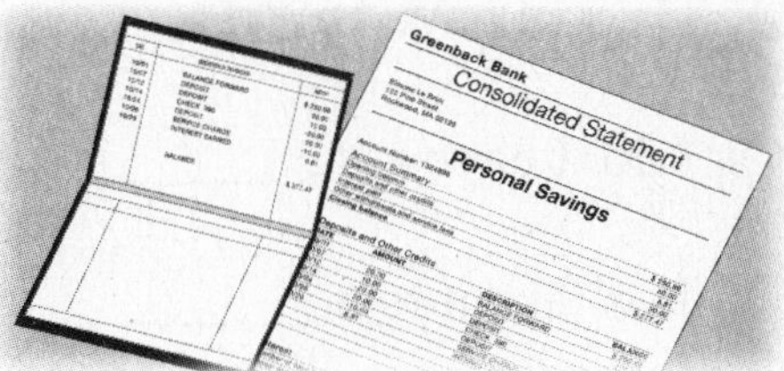

1. **a.** a joint account
   b. an individual account

2. **a.** a passbook savings account
   b. a checking account

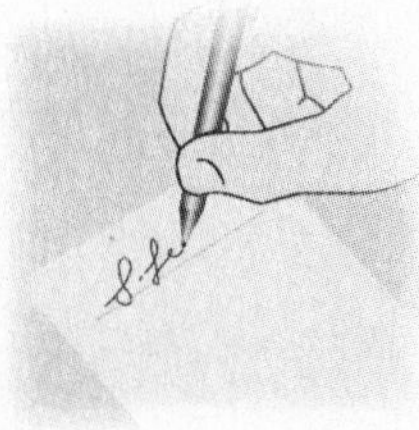

Account Summary	
Balance carried forward	$250.66
Monthly fee	$10.00
BALANCE	$240.66

3. **a.** sign a check
   b. endorse a check

4. **a.** a certificate of deposit
   b. a deposit

5. **a.** you pay the bank
   b. the bank pays you

2 **Complete the sentences. Write the letters of each word on the lines.**

1. To endorse the check, sign it on the b a c k.
2. Every month, I get a s ___ ___ ___ ___ ___ ___ ___ t from my bank.
3. Claudia has a new job at a bank. She's a b ___ ___ k t ___ ___ ___ ___ r.
4. List the checks you write in your c ___ ___ ___ ___ ___ ___ ___ k.
5. You can make a w ___ ___ ___ ___ ___ ___ ___ ___ l from your account when you need money.
6. Please write your phone number on the f ___ ___ ___ t of the check.
7. I changed banks. The fees were too h ___ ___ h at my old bank.

➤ Practical conversations

3 **Complete the conversation. Use words from the box.**

teller	endorse	right	officer
Let	savings	account	cash

A: Excuse me. I'd like to ______________ this check.
1.

B: OK. Do you have an ______________ here?
2.

A: Yes, I do. I have a ______________ account.
3.

B: OK. Just take it to a ______________. You'll need to ______________ the back.
4. 5.

A: Thanks. Can I apply for an ATM card at the window too?

B: I'm sorry. You need to fill out a form with a bank ______________.
6.

A: Can I do that right now?

B: ______________ me see. . .Well, he's not at his desk right now, but if you have a
7.

seat, he'll be ______________ with you.
8.

4 **Complete the conversations. Use your <u>own</u> words.**

1. **A:** I'm interested in ______________________________.

   B: You need to fill out this form and take it to ______________________________.

   A: Great. How long will it take?

   B: Not too long. About ______________________________.

2. **A:** I need to make a withdrawal from my ______________________________ account.

   B: OK. How much do you want to withdraw?

   A: ______________________________.

   B: And how would you like that?

   A: ______________________________, please.

Name ______________________ ID ____________ Date ____________

➤ Practical grammar

5 Complete each sentence with the superlative form of the adjective.

1. I don't want to go in Mario's car. He's ___the fastest___ (fast) driver I know. It's dangerous.
2. At this ATM, ______________ (small) withdrawal you can make is $20.
3. ______________ (important) signs here are the safety warning signs.
4. Shana is ______________ (new) employee we have; she just started last week.
5. These are ______________ (beautiful) checks we have; they have pictures of clouds on them.

6 Look at the chart. Write sentences to compare the items. Use the adjective.

1.	**February**	**June**	**December**
2.	**Mexico**	**The United States**	**Colombia**
3.	**a computer**	**a van**	**a coffee maker**
4.	**tea**	**coffee**	**orange juice**

1. (long) June is longer than February, but December is the longest.
2. (large) ______________________________
3. (expensive) ______________________________
4. (good) ______________________________

7 Complete the questions. Write the letter on the line.

1. How often ______
2. How bad ______
3. How large ______
4. How late ______
5. How low ______
6. How cold ______

a. can I pick up my car?
b. is your family?
c. do you use your credit card?
d. is the traffic in the morning?
e. is the weather today?
f. are the interest rates right now?

8 **➤ CHALLENGE** **Look at the answers. Write questions. Use <u>How</u> and a word from the box.**

expensive	interesting	dangerous	long	hot	early

1. **A:** *How early does the bank open?*
   B: The bank opens at 8:30 a.m.
2. **A:** ______________________________
   B: The weather is really hot in the summer. It's hotter than Texas.
3. **A:** ______________________________
   B: Fourth Street is not dangerous. I never see an accident there.
4. **A:** ______________________________
   B: The K-600 cameras are $299.00.
5. **A:** ______________________________
   B: It takes about 20 minutes to open a bank account.
6. **A:** ______________________________
   B: The movie was very interesting. I really liked it.

9 **➤ CHALLENGE** **Complete the conversations. Use your <u>own</u> words.**

1. **A:** What's the best drugstore in your city?
   B: ______________________________.
   A: How ____________ are the prices?
   B: They have the cheapest shampoos and soaps.

2. **A:** Who's the oldest student in your class?
   B: ______________________________.
   A: How ______________________?
   B: ______________________ years old.

3. **A:** What's the busiest street in your neighborhood?
   B: ______________________________.
   A: How ______________________?
   B: It's ____________________. I get stuck in traffic every morning.

Name ______________________ ID ______________ Date ______________

➤ Authentic practice

10 Read. Choose your response. Circle the letter.

1. "I'm really in a hurry. Will this take long?"

   a. No, not long. About ten minutes. **b.** Just take it to a teller.

2. "Make yourself comfortable. I'll only be a minute."

   a. OK. Thank you. **b.** I'll check.

3. "Which kind of account do you think is the best?"

   a. Why don't you have a seat? **b.** Let me think...

4. "Can I interest you in getting a savings club card?"

   a. How long will it take? **b.** Tens, please.

5. "Would you like that in tens or fives?"

   a. Which one pays the highest interest? **b.** Fives, please.

6. "I forgot to write the date on my check. Will that be a problem?"

   a. Don't worry. It's fine. **b.** It won't take long.

11 Put the conversation in order. Write the number on the line.

__1__ Oops. I forgot to deposit my paycheck yesterday. Did you deposit yours?

_____ That sounds great! Can anybody get direct deposit?

_____ Is it better than getting a paycheck?

_____ Actually, I don't get a paycheck.

_____ Sure. You just have to fill out an application in the Human Resources office.

_____ Because I have direct deposit, so my paycheck goes straight to my bank.

_____ You don't? Why not?

_____ Well, it's the fastest way to get your money into the bank, so it can start earning interest.

__9__ Thanks for telling me. I'll do that today.

12 Read the bank statement.

PT Prairie Trust Bank 5700 E. 8th St., Riverside, NE 68600

Lydia Markova
198 Waters St.
Riverside, NE 68600

ACCOUNT NUMBER 998724902
PERIOD COVERED October 1–October 31, 2003
page 1 of 2

Questions? Call Customer Service at 1-800-555-2985.
For information about on-line banking, call Customer Service.

PERSONAL SAVINGS

Balance at start of the period	Oct	01	$659.08
Interest	Oct	10	$1.66
Deposit	Oct	25	$50.00
Balance at close of the period	Oct	31	$710.74

PERSONAL CHECKING

Balance at start of the period	Oct	01	$524.76
Withdrawal—ATM Riverside	Oct	08	$-60.00
Deposit (pay check)	Oct	18	$374.50
Withdrawal—check #578	Oct	20	$-36.15
Withdrawal—ATM Lincoln, NE	Oct	24	$-100.00
ATM fee			$-1.00
Withdrawal—check #579	Oct	28	$-63.21
Monthly fee	Oct	31	-$5.00
Balance at close of the period	Oct	31	$633.90

4 withdrawals = $259.36 1 deposit = $374.50 2 checks cleared

Read the sentences. Check ☑ true or false.

	true	false
1. The bank statement is for two months.	❑	❑
2. Ms. Markova's balance in her checking account was higher at the end of the month than it was at the start of the month.	❑	❑
3. Ms. Markova pays a fee every month on her savings account.	❑	❑
4. She made one deposit to her savings account in October.	❑	❑
5. She used an ATM twice in October.	❑	❑
6. She cashed her paycheck on October 18.	❑	❑
7. At the end of October, she had $524.76 in her checking account.	❑	❑
8. The largest withdrawal from her checking account in October was at an ATM.	❑	❑

Name ______________________ ID ______________ Date ______________

13 **Look at Ms. Markova's check and bank documents.**

Lydia Markova
198 Waters St.
Riverside, NE 68600

580

DATE 11/01/03

PAY TO THE ORDER OF Selena Ochoa $ 75.00

Seventy-five and 00/100 DOLLARS

Prairie Trust Bank
5700 E. 8th St.
Riverside, NE 68600

FOR child care

Lydia Markova

|:0 20663973|: 3322883327: 580

PT Prairie Trust Bank

LOCATION	DATE	TIME
RS 1250	Nov 06, 03	10:30 a.m.

TRANSACTION	AMOUNT
Withdrawal from checking	$80.00

No fee: first ATM withdrawal of the month is free.

Lydia Markova
198 Waters St.
Riverside, NE 68600

DEPOSIT SLIP

Please fill out this ticket before you advance to the teller's window.
For mail-in or ATM deposits, enclose this slip in the envelope with your deposit.

Date: 11/04/03

Your deposit may not be immediately available for withdrawal.

Account to which you want this deposit posted:

❑ savings ☑ checking ❑ holiday savings club

PT Prairie Trust Bank
5700 E. 8th St., Riverside, NE 68600

Cash		
Check paycheck	389.	00
Check		
Check		
Subtotal		
Less cash received		
Net deposit	389.	00

Now enter the transactions for the activity on November 1, 4, and 6 in Ms. Markova's check register.

Check number	Date	Trans type	Transaction Description	Withdrawal (–) (payment/ debit)		Fee	Tax Ex?	Deposit (+) (credit/ payment)		Balance	
										524	76
-	10/8	ATM	withdrawal	60	00	-				-60	00
										464	76
-	10/18	-	paycheck					374	50	+374	50
										839	26
578	10/20	-	Riverside Gas and	36	15					-36	15
			Electric utility bill							803	11
-	10/24	ATM	withdrawal	100	00					-100	00
			fee			1.00				-1	00
										702	11
579	10/28	-	Food City groceries	63	21					-63	21
										638	90
-	10/31	-	Monthly checking fee							-5	00
										633	90

14 **Read the bank officer's words. Then fill in the chart.**

Our Type 1 CD is our fastest. It's a 6-month CD, and it pays 3.5% interest. To get a higher interest rate, you have to leave your money in the CD longer. Our Type 2 CD is a 1-year CD, and it pays 4%. Our Type 3 CD matures in 2 years and pays 4.75%. Our highest interest rate is on our Type 4, 3-year CD; it pays 5.5%. You should choose the CD that's best for you.

Type	Length of time to mature	Interest paid
1	6 months	
2		
3		
4		

15 **➤CHALLENGE** **Lydia Markova's employers offer direct deposit to their employees. Look at Ms. Markova's direct deposit application.**

Fill in this information about yourself.

Employee's name: Lydia Markova

Department: Accounting

Fill in this information about the financial institution to which you would like your paycheck deposited.

Name of your bank or credit union: Prairie Trust Bank

Account number: 998724902 Type of account: ☐ savings ☑ checking

You need to attach a blank, voided check from your account to this application.
The direct deposit will start after approximately one month.

Read the answers. Then complete the questions.

1. **A:** What is ______________________________?

   B: It's 998724902.

2. **A:** ______________________________ Ms. Markova work?

   B: In the accounting department.

3. **A:** ______________________________ for the direct deposit to start?

   B: About a month.

4. **A:** ______________________________ to attach to her application?

   B: A blank, voided check from her account.

Name ______________________ ID __________ Date __________

UNIT 10

Your career

Vocabulary

1 Complete the sentences. Write the letter on the line.

1. Ms. Maldonado is working at Beta Computer. She's ______.
2. Mr. Loyola's wife and children are also covered by his health insurance. They're his ______.
3. To get a ______, fill out the claim form and send it to the insurance company.
4. The Kaplans are taking a trip to Hawaii for their next ______.
5. The company has a good ______ plan for its employees' retirement.
6. Ms. Han just got a promotion. She's an assistant manager now, and her ______ is higher.
7. Mr. Leonowicz has his own business. He's ________.
8. Under this medical plan, employees will pay a small _______ when they have a doctor's appointment.
9. I'm looking for a job. I'm _______ right now.

a. vacation
b. pension
c. co-payment
d. salary
e. unemployed
f. reimbursement
g. self-employed
h. employed
i. dependents

2 Complete the chart. Use your own words.

Benefits I have	Benefits I would like to have

➤ Practical conversations

3 **Complete the conversations. Use words from the box.**

yet	don't	been	kidding	since
Guess	haven't	supposed	dental	signed up

1. **A:** When are we ____________ to get our insurance cards?
   1.

   B: It usually takes about three weeks. Why?

   A: Well, I ____________ last month, and I ____________
   2. 3.

   gotten my card ____________.
   4.

   B: Why ____________ you ask in the Benefits office?
   5.

   A: I will. Thanks.

2. **A:** ____________ what! We're going to have a ____________
   6. 7.

   plan next year!

   B: No ____________! That's wonderful. My husband is self-
   8.

   employed, so I really need good benefits.

   A: How long has he ____________ self-employed?
   9.

   B: Just ____________ March.
   10.

4 **Complete the conversations. Use your <u>own</u> words.**

1. **A:** Do you have good benefits where you work?

   B: Yes, we do. We have a fantastic ____________, and a good ____________ too.

   A: Can you choose the ____________ you like?

   B: Yes, we can.

2. **A:** How long have you worked here?

   B: Since ____________. Why?

   A: Can you tell me when we're supposed to sign up for ____________?

   B: Sure. You need to sign up ____________.

Name ______________________ ID ____________ Date ____________

➤ Practical grammar

5 **Complete the sentences. Use the present perfect.**

1. I ___have___ already ___taken___ (take) two personal days this year.
2. We__________ (be) really busy today, but I __________ (not forget) about your question.
3. __________ Susan __________ (leave) yet? I wanted to talk to her.
4. I __________ only __________ (withdraw) $25 from that account since I opened it.
5. I __________ (know) Maria since we were children.
6. __________ you __________ (get) your reimbursement from the insurance company yet?
7. Henri needs a vacation! He __________ (not have) one in three years!
8. __________ your father __________ (make) an appointment with the optician yet?

6 **Complete the sentences. Use already, yet, for, or since.**

1. I've ___already___ chosen a doctor, but I haven't chosen a dentist ___yet___.
2. Mrs. Ruiz has been unemployed __________ about two months.
3. Long time, no see! I haven't seen you __________ last year!
4. Has the new sick leave policy started __________?
5. Before he retired, Toshi worked in the same office __________ 35 years.
6. Larry just got this job yesterday, and he's __________ broken two rules.
7. Where have you been __________ 9:00?
8. You'd better hurry! It's 7:00 and your shift has __________ started!

7 **Look at Roxana Lopez's date book for today. It's 2:30 p.m. Write sentences about what she has already done and what she hasn't done yet.**

15
OCTOBER

✓ 7:30 a.m. —drop off the car
✓ 9:00 a.m.—go to the post office
✓ 12:00 a.m.—have lunch with Lydia
3:00 p.m.—go to computer training class
5:30 p.m.—pick up the car
8:30 p.m.—do the laundry

1. *She has already dropped off the car.*
2. ______________________________
3. ______________________________
4. ______________________________
5. ______________________________
6. ______________________________

8 ➤***CHALLENGE*** **Put the words in order to make sentences or questions.**

1. these claim forms / we / fill out / When / supposed to / are

   ______________________________?

2. Why / ask about / the medical plan / at the interview / don't you

   ______________________________?

3. now / give / Am / you / my co-payment / I / supposed to

   ______________________________?

4. ask / Why / the office manager / pension plans / don't we / about

   ______________________________?

5. sign up for / I / a benefits meeting, / but / forgot / was supposed to / I

   ______________________________.

9 **Answer the questions. Use the present of be supposed to and your own words.**

1. What are you supposed to do if you want to take a vacation from work?

   ____

2. What are you not supposed to do in your English class?

   ____

Name ________________________ ID ______________ Date ______________

➤ Authentic practice

10 **Read. Choose your response. Circle the letter.**

1. "Can I list my mother as my dependent?"

   a. Why don't you sign up? **b.** Why don't you check in the office?

2. "The company closed, and my dad got laid off."

   a. No, I don't. **b.** Oh, no.

3. "Guess what Levi told me!"

   a. What? **b.** That's fantastic!

4. "I heard we're supposed to choose a new plan by this Friday."

   a. No kidding. That's not much time. **b.** No, I haven't. Not yet.

5. "What if I break the rules?"

   a. I'm not sure. **b.** That's great.

6. "Where have you looked for a job?"

   a. Since last week. **b.** Actually, I haven't started yet.

11 **Read the conversation.**

Joy: Luigi! How's it going? I haven't seen you since I left that job at Post Plus.

Luigi: You're right. Long time, no see! How have you been?

Joy: Not bad. How about you?

Luigi: OK. I still work in the engineering department. I'm the manager now.

Joy: No kidding! How long have you been there?

Luigi: This is my 14th year.

Joy: Wow! You know, I left Post Plus because they didn't offer health insurance. Have the benefits gotten any better?

Luigi: Yes, they have. We have a health plan and a dental plan now.

Joy: Great! I'm going to get a cup of coffee. Why don't you come with me?

Luigi: I'd like to, but I can't. I'm supposed to meet my wife, and I'm already late.

Joy: OK. Well, I'd better let you go. It was great seeing you!

Luigi: Great seeing you too.

Look at the sentences. Check ☑ yes, no, or I don't know.

	yes	no	I don't know
1. Joy works at Post Plus.	❑	❑	❑
2. Luigi works at Post Plus.	❑	❑	❑
3. Joy hasn't seen Luigi for 10 years.	❑	❑	❑
4. The benefits at Post Plus have gotten better.	❑	❑	❑
5. Luigi changed jobs after Joy left Post Plus.	❑	❑	❑
6. Luigi has worked at Post Plus for 4 years.	❑	❑	❑
7. Luigi has been the manager for 14 months.	❑	❑	❑
8. Joy asks Luigi to have dinner with her.	❑	❑	❑
9. Luigi can't have coffee because he has to work.	❑	❑	❑

12 **Look at today's work schedule for the Regal Motel. Then answer the questions.**

REGAL MOTEL — **WORK SCHEDULE** — Tuesday, July 18th

	Misha Karkov	Phu Nguyen	Leti Saavedra
8:00 a.m.–10:00 a.m.	clean lobby and parking lot	clean 2nd floor rooms	make breakfast; clean breakfast room
10:00 a.m.–12:00 p.m.	do laundry	clean 2nd floor rooms	clean 3rd floor rooms
12:30 p.m.–2:30 p.m.	clean 1st floor rooms	do laundry	clean 3rd floor rooms
2:30 p.m.–4:30 p.m.	clean 1st floor rooms	clean laundry room and pool area	do laundry

1. It's 9:00 a.m. Has Mr. Karkov done any laundry yet? ____________________
2. It's 10:30 a.m. Has Ms. Saavedra cleaned the breakfast room yet? ____________________
3. It's 2:15 p.m. Has Ms. Nguyen cleaned the laundry room yet? ____________________
4. It's 3:00 p.m. Are the rooms on the third floor clean? ____________________
5. It's 12:00 noon. What has Ms. Nguyen already done? ____________________

____

Name ______________________ ID ____________ Date ____________

➤ Authentic practice

13 Look at the poster. Then answer the questions.

Employee Benefits Fair

Date: Friday, May 6th
Time: 10:00 a.m. to 4:00 p.m.
Place: Cafeteria

Advisors will be available to answer questions about benefits. Sign up in the Human Resources office by Wednesday, May 4th at 5:00. Call Pam Jackson at extension 5136.

1. When are employees supposed to sign up for the benefits fair? ______________
2. Where are they supposed to sign up? ______________
3. Who are they supposed to call? ______________
4. Where are they supposed to go for the benefits fair? ______________

14 ➤ *CHALLENGE* Read François Fleur's pay stub. Then complete the paragraph.

Super Auto

François Fleur
6/22/03
Check # 38059

Earnings		Deductions	Amount		
Gross pay	$618.30	Federal Tax	$49.10	Pay date	6/22/03
Hours	80	State Tax	$37.55	Pay begin date	6/6/03
		Medicare Tax	$8.53	Pay end date	6/20/03
		Soc Sec Tax	$37.10		

Net Pay $486.02 Total Deductions $132.28

Year-to-Date	Amount
Gross pay	$7,423.60
Federal Tax	$589.50
State Tax	$450.84
Medicare Tax	$102.41
Soc Sec Tax	$445.44

François Fleur works at ______ (1.). He got a paycheck on ______ (2.). The paycheck covers ______ (3.) weeks. The pay period began on ______ (4.) and ended on June 20. During the pay period, Mr. Fleur worked ______ (5.) hours. His ______ (6.) pay was $618.30. He had $132.28 in ______ (7.), or money taken out of his gross pay. $86.65 of the deductions was for ______ (8.) and state taxes. Mr. Fleur's ______ (9.) pay was $486.02. Since the beginning of this ______ (10.), Mr. Fleur has earned $7,423.60. So far in 2003, he has paid ______ (11.) in Social Security tax.

15 **Nuria Abdi works full-time at Super Auto and is eligible for benefits. She has filled out the first part of the benefits application. Read the form.**

Super Auto | **Benefits Enrollment Form**

Please check the type(s) of benefits for which you are applying:

❑ Health Plan only ☑ Health Plan with Dental Plan

❑ Health Plan with Vision Plan ❑ Health Plan with Dental and Vision Plans

Have you chosen a primary care doctor yet? ❑ no ☑ yes: Dr. Pamela Hassan

Yourself

Name: Abdi (Last) Nuria (First) Ahmed (Middle)

Date of birth: 1 / 1 / 74 (m d y) Sex: ❑ M ☑ F Department: Customer Service

Your dependents (include your spouse and dependent children under the age of 18 only)

Name: ______ Last ______ First ______ Middle

Date of birth: ____/____/____ (m d y) Sex: ❑ M ❑ F

Relationship to employee: ______________

Name: ______ Last ______ First ______ Middle

Date of birth: ____/____/____ (m d y) Sex: ❑ M ❑ F

Relationship to employee: ______________

Ms. Abdi would like to enroll her husband and daughter in her health plan. Complete her conversation with the Human Resources manager. Then fill in the form for her dependents.

1. **Manager:** ____?

   Ms. Abdi: His name is Yassin Tayeb. He doesn't have a middle name.

2. **Manager:** ____?

   Ms. Abdi: March 6, 1975.

3. **Manager:** ____?

   Ms. Abdi: Her name is Aisha Nur Tayeb.

4. **Manager:** ____?

   Ms. Abdi: August 29, 2002.

Answer the questions. Use your <u>own</u> words.

1. How long have you been a student at your school?

   ____

2. How long have you known your best friend?

   ____

Skills for test taking

Write your information in the boxes. Fill in the ovals.

LAST NAME															FIRST NAME															MI
A	A	A	A	A	A	A	A	A	A	A	A	A	A	A	A	A	A	A	A	A	A	A	A	A	A	A	A	A	A	A
B	B	B	B	B	B	B	B	B	B	B	B	B	B	B	B	B	B	B	B	B	B	B	B	B	B	B	B	B	B	B
C	C	C	C	C	C	C	C	C	C	C	C	C	C	C	C	C	C	C	C	C	C	C	C	C	C	C	C	C	C	C
D	D	D	D	D	D	D	D	D	D	D	D	D	D	D	D	D	D	D	D	D	D	D	D	D	D	D	D	D	D	D
E	E	E	E	E	E	E	E	E	E	E	E	E	E	E	E	E	E	E	E	E	E	E	E	E	E	E	E	E	E	E
F	F	F	F	F	F	F	F	F	F	F	F	F	F	F	F	F	F	F	F	F	F	F	F	F	F	F	F	F	F	F
G	G	G	G	G	G	G	G	G	G	G	G	G	G	G	G	G	G	G	G	G	G	G	G	G	G	G	G	G	G	G
H	H	H	H	H	H	H	H	H	H	H	H	H	H	H	H	H	H	H	H	H	H	H	H	H	H	H	H	H	H	H
I	I	I	I	I	I	I	I	I	I	I	I	I	I	I	I	I	I	I	I	I	I	I	I	I	I	I	I	I	I	I
J	J	J	J	J	J	J	J	J	J	J	J	J	J	J	J	J	J	J	J	J	J	J	J	J	J	J	J	J	J	J
K	K	K	K	K	K	K	K	K	K	K	K	K	K	K	K	K	K	K	K	K	K	K	K	K	K	K	K	K	K	K
L	L	L	L	L	L	L	L	L	L	L	L	L	L	L	L	L	L	L	L	L	L	L	L	L	L	L	L	L	L	L
M	M	M	M	M	M	M	M	M	M	M	M	M	M	M	M	M	M	M	M	M	M	M	M	M	M	M	M	M	M	M
N	N	N	N	N	N	N	N	N	N	N	N	N	N	N	N	N	N	N	N	N	N	N	N	N	N	N	N	N	N	N
O	O	O	O	O	O	O	O	O	O	O	O	O	O	O	O	O	O	O	O	O	O	O	O	O	O	O	O	O	O	O
P	P	P	P	P	P	P	P	P	P	P	P	P	P	P	P	P	P	P	P	P	P	P	P	P	P	P	P	P	P	P
Q	Q	Q	Q	Q	Q	Q	Q	Q	Q	Q	Q	Q	Q	Q	Q	Q	Q	Q	Q	Q	Q	Q	Q	Q	Q	Q	Q	Q	Q	Q
R	R	R	R	R	R	R	R	R	R	R	R	R	R	R	R	R	R	R	R	R	R	R	R	R	R	R	R	R	R	R
S	S	S	S	S	S	S	S	S	S	S	S	S	S	S	S	S	S	S	S	S	S	S	S	S	S	S	S	S	S	S
T	T	T	T	T	T	T	T	T	T	T	T	T	T	T	T	T	T	T	T	T	T	T	T	T	T	T	T	T	T	T
U	U	U	U	U	U	U	U	U	U	U	U	U	U	U	U	U	U	U	U	U	U	U	U	U	U	U	U	U	U	U
V	V	V	V	V	V	V	V	V	V	V	V	V	V	V	V	V	V	V	V	V	V	V	V	V	V	V	V	V	V	V
W	W	W	W	W	W	W	W	W	W	W	W	W	W	W	W	W	W	W	W	W	W	W	W	W	W	W	W	W	W	W
X	X	X	X	X	X	X	X	X	X	X	X	X	X	X	X	X	X	X	X	X	X	X	X	X	X	X	X	X	X	X
Y	Y	Y	Y	Y	Y	Y	Y	Y	Y	Y	Y	Y	Y	Y	Y	Y	Y	Y	Y	Y	Y	Y	Y	Y	Y	Y	Y	Y	Y	Y
Z	Z	Z	Z	Z	Z	Z	Z	Z	Z	Z	Z	Z	Z	Z	Z	Z	Z	Z	Z	Z	Z	Z	Z	Z	Z	Z	Z	Z	Z	Z

DATE OF BIRTH				
Month	Day		Year 19__	
Jan	0	0	0	0
Feb	1	1	1	1
Mar	2	2	2	2
Apr	3	3	3	3
May		4	4	4
Jun		5	5	5
Jul		6	6	6
Aug		7	7	7
Sep		8	8	8
Oct		9	9	9
Nov				
Dec				

TELEPHONE NUMBER									
0	0	0	0	0	0	0	0	0	0
1	1	1	1	1	1	1	1	1	1
2	2	2	2	2	2	2	2	2	2
3	3	3	3	3	3	3	3	3	3
4	4	4	4	4	4	4	4	4	4
5	5	5	5	5	5	5	5	5	5
6	6	6	6	6	6	6	6	6	6
7	7	7	7	7	7	7	7	7	7
8	8	8	8	8	8	8	8	8	8
9	9	9	9	9	9	9	9	9	9

TODAY'S DATE				
Month	Day		Year 20__	
Jan	0	0	0	0
Feb	1	1	1	1
Mar	2	2	2	2
Apr	3	3		3
May		4		4
Jun		5		5
Jul		6		6
Aug		7		7
Sep		8		8
Oct		9		9
Nov				
Dec				

Name ______________________ ID ____________ Date ____________

Unit 1

Choose an answer.

To: Vilma Gutierrez
Date: 11/6/02 Time: 11:30 a.m. ☑ p.m. ☐

WHILE YOU WERE OUT

(Mr.)/Ms. Adam Latour
Phone: 555-1804

☑ telephoned ☐ please call
☐ returned your call ☑ will call back

Message taken by: Ryan Clark

1. Who left a message?

   A. Ms. Gutierrez.
   B. Mr. Latour.
   C. Mr. Clark.
   D. We don't know.

2. When did Mr. Latour call?

   A. On June 11.
   B. On November 2.
   C. At 11:30 a.m.
   D. At 11:30 p.m.

3. Who will call?

   A. Vilma Gutierrez will call Adam Latour.
   B. Adam Latour will call Vilma Gutierrez.
   C. Ryan Clark will call Vilma Gutierrez.
   D. Vilma Gutierrez will call Ryan Clark.

1. Ⓐ Ⓑ Ⓒ Ⓓ

2. Ⓐ Ⓑ Ⓒ Ⓓ

3. Ⓐ Ⓑ Ⓒ Ⓓ

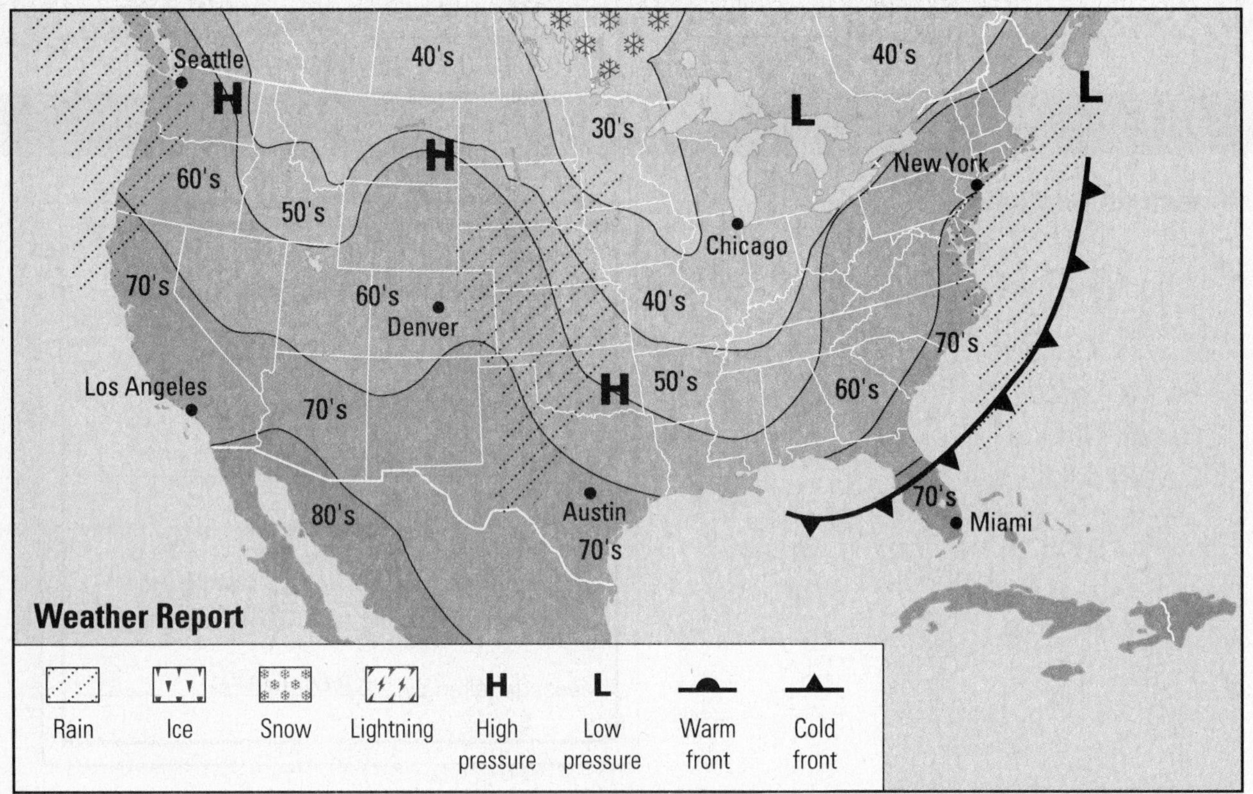

4. A. It's warm in Los Angeles.
   B. It's cool in Los Angeles.
   C. It's raining in Los Angeles.
   D. It's cold in Los Angeles.

5. A. You'll need an umbrella in Miami.
   B. You'll need a coat in Los Angeles.
   C. You'll need a coat in Austin.
   D. You'll need a raincoat in Seattle.

4. Ⓐ Ⓑ Ⓒ Ⓓ

5. Ⓐ Ⓑ Ⓒ Ⓓ

Name ______________________ ID ____________ Date ____________

Unit 2

Choose an answer.

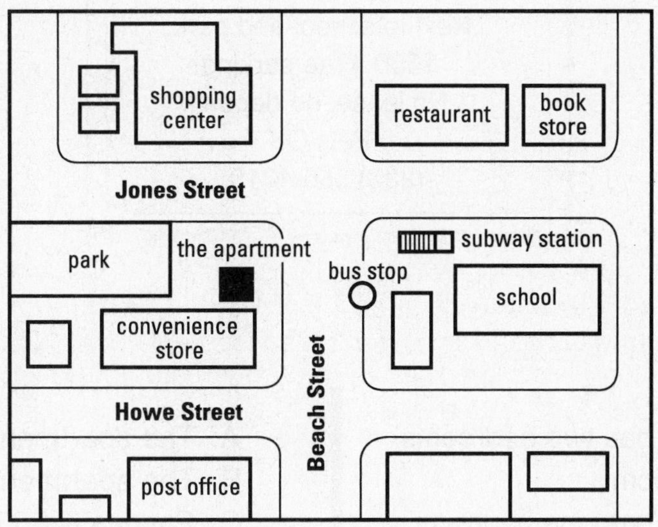

1. Where is the apartment?

   A. It's next door to the school.
   B. It's down the street from the bus stop.
   C. It's across the street from the bus stop.
   D. It's around the corner from the subway station.

2. What's next to the restaurant?

   A. The bus stop.
   B. The school.
   C. The book store.
   D. The restaurant.

1. Ⓐ Ⓑ Ⓒ Ⓓ

2. Ⓐ Ⓑ Ⓒ Ⓓ

FOR RENT

TWIN CITY

Sm. 2-bdrm,
1-bath apartment; 3rd floor.
Next to school and park.
$500. Free parking.
No lease, no deposit.
Pets OK.
(233) 555-4019.

3. A. The apartment has two bedrooms and one bathroom.
   B. The apartment has one bedroom and one bathroom.
   C. The apartment has a large bedroom.
   D. The apartment is in the basement.

4. A. The deposit is one month's rent.
   B. The deposit is two months' rent.
   C. There is a lease.
   D. There isn't a deposit.

5. A. The apartment is near a park.
   B. The apartment is in a park.
   C. Parking is $500.
   D. The apartment doesn't have parking.

3. Ⓐ Ⓑ Ⓒ Ⓓ

4. Ⓐ Ⓑ Ⓒ Ⓓ

5. Ⓐ Ⓑ Ⓒ Ⓓ

Name ______________________ ID ____________ Date ____________

Unit 3

Choose an answer.

UNIVERSAL
CARS AND TRUCKS

Describe problem

I was driving home last night and the "Check Engine" light came on. Now it won't go off. Rear right door won't close.

Repair/Service Work Order

NAME	DATE
Therese Louis	January 17, 2003
ADDRESS 149 East 19th Street Apt. #2	
Fort Worth, TX 79702	
PHONE NUMBER (217) 555-1392	
MODEL AND YEAR 2000 Hurricane SE	LICENSE PLATE NUMBER AVM 450

Estimate	Drop-off time	Pick-up time
$90 00	8:45 a.m.	4:00 p.m (will call first)

1. What are the problems with Ms. Louis's car?
   A. The "Check Engine" warning light won't go off and two doors won't open.
   B. The windshield wipers aren't working and one door won't open.
   C. The "Check Engine" warning light won't go off and one door won't close.
   D. The turn signals won't go on and one door won't close.

2. When did Ms. Louis drop off her car?
   A. 4:00 a.m.
   B. 4:00 p.m.
   C. 8:45 a.m.
   D. 8:45 p.m.

3. What was Ms. Louis doing when the problem started?
   A. She was driving home.
   B. She was driving to the garage.
   C. She was driving to work.
   D. She was calling the garage.

1. Ⓐ Ⓑ Ⓒ Ⓓ

2. Ⓐ Ⓑ Ⓒ Ⓓ

3. Ⓐ Ⓑ Ⓒ Ⓓ

Stacie,

Can you please look at the copier? It wasn't working when I came in this morning. The "Check Paper" light was on, and I filled it up with paper, but the light won't go off. I turned the copier off, and then I turned it on again, but it won't start.

Thanks,

Tigist

4. A. Tigist filled the copier up with gas.
   B. Stacie turned the copier off.
   C. Stacie filled the copier up with paper.
   D. Tigist filled the copier up with paper.

5. A. The copier won't start.
   B. The copier won't go off.
   C. The copier was working when Tigist came in.
   D. The "Check Paper" light was off when Tigist came in.

4. Ⓐ Ⓑ Ⓒ Ⓓ

5. Ⓐ Ⓑ Ⓒ Ⓓ

Name ______________________ ID ____________ Date ____________

Unit 4

Choose an answer.

1. A. The store brand film is cheaper than Presto film.
   B. The store brand film is more expensive than Presto film.
   C. $3.99 is the price for Presto film.
   D. Presto film is cheaper than the store brand film.

2. A. Tissues aren't on sale.
   B. Mr. Ishi paid $1.98 for two boxes of Softy tissues on July 7. He was overcharged.
   C. A box of 200 Walbert's tissues is cheaper than a box of 100 Softy tissues.
   D. Tissues are on sale. The store brand ones are $.99.

3. A. Thermometers are on sale for $3.99.
   B. The sale price for Walbert's shampoo is $1.99.
   C. The sale prices are good for one week.
   D. The store brand film isn't on sale.

1. Ⓐ Ⓑ Ⓒ Ⓓ

2. Ⓐ Ⓑ Ⓒ Ⓓ

3. Ⓐ Ⓑ Ⓒ Ⓓ

Date *10/15/03*

Sold-out item *Star XP 500 flash camera*

Color *silver*

Sale price *$29.99*

Good until *11/15/03*

4. When did the salesperson write the rain check?

   A. October 12, 2003.
   B. October 19, 2003.
   C. October 15, 2003.
   D. November 15, 2003.

5. How long is the rain check good for?

   A. One week.
   B. One month.
   C. Two months.
   D. Three months.

4. Ⓐ Ⓑ Ⓒ Ⓓ

5. Ⓐ Ⓑ Ⓒ Ⓓ

Name ______________________ ID ____________ Date ____________

Unit 5

Choose an answer.

Yorktown Bus Route Schedule

Type	Yorktown Mall	46th St.	31st St.	16th St.	Center City
local	7:05 a.m.	7:19 a.m.	7:29 a.m.	7:39 a.m.	7:45 a.m.
local	7:35 a.m.	7:49 a.m.	7:59 a.m.	8:09 a.m.	8:15 a.m.
express	8:00 a.m.	-------	-------	-------	8:30 a.m.
local	8:05 a.m.	8:19 a.m.	8:29 a.m.	8:39 a.m.	8:45 a.m.

1. Brenda is at Yorktown Mall. She wants to arrive at the Center City stop before 8:00 a.m. She should take the ________.

   A. 7:05 bus
   B. 7:35 bus
   C. 8:00 bus
   D. 8:05 bus

2. The 7:35 bus from Yorktown Mall arrives at the 46th St. stop at ________.

   A. 7:19 a.m.
   B. 7:29 a.m.
   C. 7:49 a.m.
   D. 7:59 a.m.

3. In the morning, the local bus from Yorktown Mall leaves every ________.

   A. 10 minutes
   B. 12 minutes
   C. 30 minutes
   D. hour

1. Ⓐ Ⓑ Ⓒ Ⓓ

2. Ⓐ Ⓑ Ⓒ Ⓓ

3. Ⓐ Ⓑ Ⓒ Ⓓ

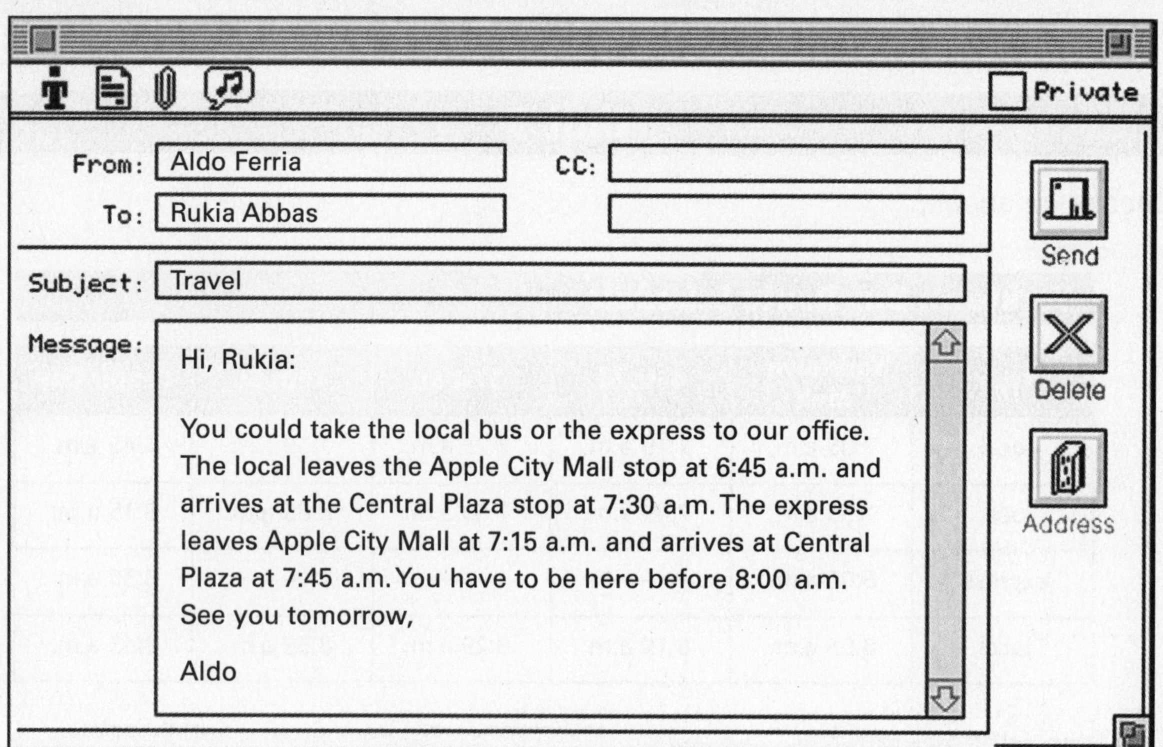

Hi, Rukia:

You could take the local bus or the express to our office. The local leaves the Apple City Mall stop at 6:45 a.m. and arrives at the Central Plaza stop at 7:30 a.m. The express leaves Apple City Mall at 7:15 a.m. and arrives at Central Plaza at 7:45 a.m. You have to be here before 8:00 a.m.
See you tomorrow,

Aldo

4. The express bus arrives at Central Plaza ________.

   A. at 7:15 a.m.
   B. at 7:45 a.m.
   C. at 8:00 a.m.
   D. after 8:00 a.m.

5. Rukia arrived at the Apple City Mall stop at 6:50 a.m. She ________.

   A. could take the local bus at 7:15 a.m.
   B. could take the 6:45 local bus
   C. couldn't take the 7:15 express
   D. just missed the local bus

4. Ⓐ Ⓑ Ⓒ Ⓓ

5. Ⓐ Ⓑ Ⓒ Ⓓ

Name ______________________ ID ______________ Date ______________

Unit 6

Choose an answer.

Kirbie's Restaurants
SUPPLY WAREHOUSE — Supply Requisition Form

Location: Aster Street Restaurant — Today's date: 6/25/03

Person filling in this form: Ly Tran

Item	Quantity	Item	Quantity
liquid soap	2 boxes	paper towels	4 cartons
tissues	4 cartons	trash bags, small	1 carton
kitchen cleanser	1 carton	trash bags, large	2 cartons

1. Who ordered the supplies?
   A. Ms. Kirbie.
   B. Aster Street.
   C. Ly Tran.
   D. The supply warehouse.

2. When did she order the supplies?
   A. At the warehouse.
   B. On June 25.
   C. At the Aster Street Restaurant.
   D. Tomorrow morning.

3. How many trash bags did she order?
   A. We don't know.
   B. Three trash bags.
   C. Three cartons.
   D. Two trash bags.

1. Ⓐ Ⓑ Ⓒ Ⓓ

2. Ⓐ Ⓑ Ⓒ Ⓓ

3. Ⓐ Ⓑ Ⓒ Ⓓ

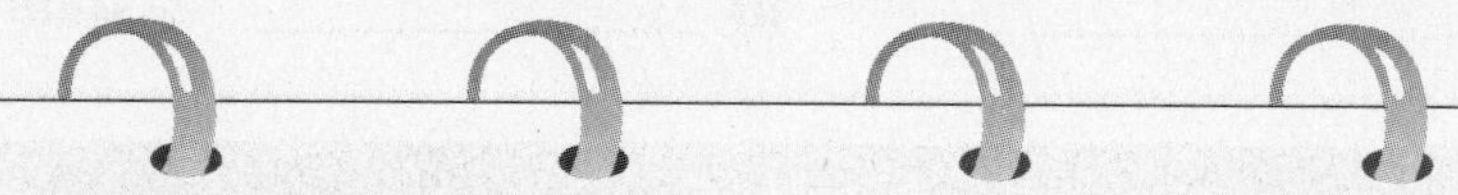

The Wilton Towers

Housekeepers' Supply Checklist

Stock the following for each bathroom:

Item	Quantity
mini shampoo	1
mini conditioner	1
body lotion	1
bath soap	1

Item	Quantity
face soap	1
washcloths	2
bath towels	2
face towels	2

EVERY DAY **Change sheets and towels.**
Replace personal care products. Empty trash.

4. A. Housekeepers need to put supplies in every bathroom.
   B. Housekeepers need to put five towels in every bathroom.
   C. Housekeepers don't need to put any soap in the bathrooms.
   D. Housekeepers need to put sponges in every bathroom.

5. A. Housekeepers don't have to change the sheets.
   B. Housekeepers have to make the beds every week.
   C. Housekeepers don't empty the trash.
   D. Housekeepers have to put clean towels in every bathroom.

4. Ⓐ Ⓑ Ⓒ Ⓓ

5. Ⓐ Ⓑ Ⓒ Ⓓ

Name ______________________ ID ______________ Date ______________

Unit 7

Choose an answer.

Townsend Industries

Medical Emergency Leave Policy

You may take medical emergency leave if you or a member of your family (your child, husband, wife, or parent) is sick or has an injury or medical emergency. Please call the personnel manager before 7 a.m. if you need to take a medical emergency leave. You will need to fill out an emergency leave form when you return to work.

17

1. Nancy Bodre wants to take medical emergency leave. What does she have to do?
   A. Call her doctor and call the personnel manager.
   B. Fill out a doctor's report.
   C. Call her personnel manager and fill out a form.
   D. Ask her doctor to call her manager.

2. When should employees call if they need to take medical emergency leave?
   A. Before 7 a.m.
   B. After 7 a.m.
   C. One day before they are sick.
   D. When they return to work.

3. Ermal Turkesi is a Townsend Industries employee. Who could he take medical emergency leave for?
   A. His son-in-law.
   B. His grandmother.
   C. His brother-in-law.
   D. His daughter.

1. Ⓐ Ⓑ Ⓒ Ⓓ

2. Ⓐ Ⓑ Ⓒ Ⓓ

3. Ⓐ Ⓑ Ⓒ Ⓓ

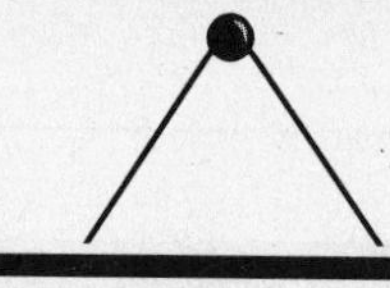

It is against the
rules to send or
get personal
e-mails at work.

4. A. It's against the rules to smoke outside the building.
   B. It's OK to smoke in the building.
   C. It's against the rules to smoke in the building.
   D. Employees had better smoke in the building.

5. A. If you send a personal e-mail or smoke in the building, you'll break the rules.
   B. It's OK to get personal e-mails at work.
   C. If you get personal e-mails, you'll get a promotion.
   D. It's OK to send personal e-mails, but smoking is against the rules.

4. Ⓐ Ⓑ Ⓒ Ⓓ

5. Ⓐ Ⓑ Ⓒ Ⓓ

Name ______________________ ID ____________ Date ____________

Unit 8

Choose an answer.

Sign 1

Sign 2

Sign 3

Sign 4

1. Which warning sign should you use if there is water on the floor?
   A. Sign 1.
   B. Sign 2.
   C. Sign 3.
   D. Sign 4.

2. Where might you see sign 2?
   A. In a parking lot.
   B. In a kitchen.
   C. In a bathroom.
   D. At a bus stop.

1. Ⓐ Ⓑ Ⓒ Ⓓ

2. Ⓐ Ⓑ Ⓒ Ⓓ

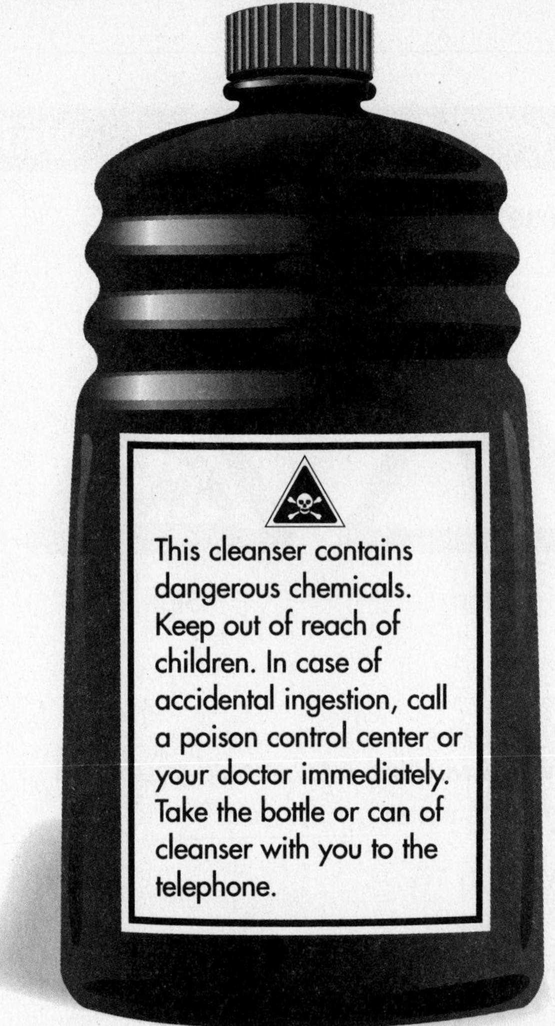

This cleanser contains
dangerous chemicals.
Keep out of reach of
children. In case of
accidental ingestion, call
a poison control center or
your doctor immediately.
Take the bottle or can of
cleanser with you to the
telephone.

3. A. This warning is on a fire extinguisher.
   B. This warning is on a bottle of cleanser.
   C. This warning is on a smoke detector.
   D. This warning is on a fire alarm.

4. A. If you drink this cleanser, you might get sick.
   B. If children drink this cleaner, they might get a shock.
   C. If you drink this cleanser, you should call the doctor tomorrow.
   D. If you use this cleanser, you will get sick.

5. A. You should take the cleanser to the doctor.
   B. You should give this cleanser to your children.
   C. You should call your doctor before you use this cleanser.
   D. Children should not use this cleanser.

3. Ⓐ Ⓑ Ⓒ Ⓓ

4. Ⓐ Ⓑ Ⓒ Ⓓ

5. Ⓐ Ⓑ Ⓒ Ⓓ

Name ______________________ ID ____________ Date ____________

Unit 9

Choose an answer.

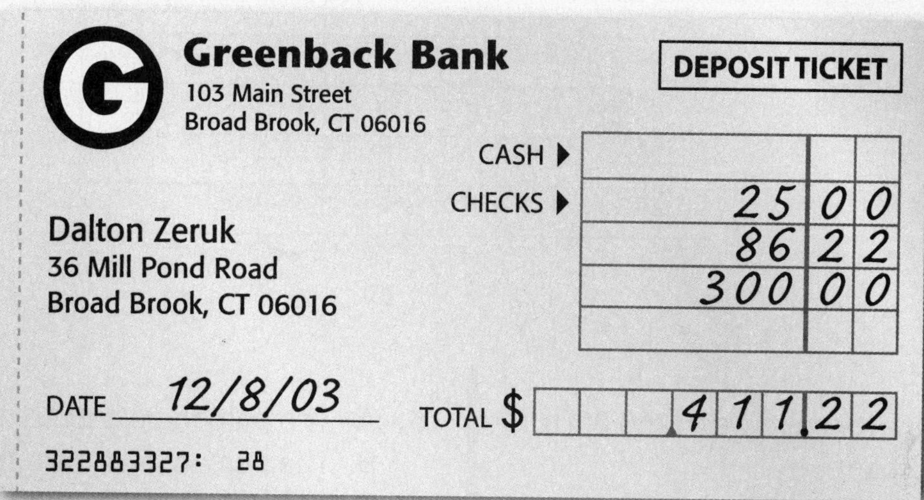

Greenback Bank
103 Main Street
Broad Brook, CT 06016

DEPOSIT TICKET

Dalton Zeruk
36 Mill Pond Road
Broad Brook, CT 06016

CASH		
CHECKS	25	00
	86	22
	300	00

DATE 12/8/03

TOTAL $ 411.22

322883327: 28

1. This bank document is a ________.
   - A. withdrawal slip
   - B. check register
   - C. deposit slip
   - D. bank statement

2. Mr. Zeruk made a deposit on ________.
   - A. August 13
   - B. August 12
   - C. March 8
   - D. December 8

3. Mr. Zeruk made a total deposit of ________.
   - A. $25.00
   - B. $86.22
   - C. $411.22
   - D. $300.00

1. Ⓐ Ⓑ Ⓒ Ⓓ

2. Ⓐ Ⓑ Ⓒ Ⓓ

3. Ⓐ Ⓑ Ⓒ Ⓓ

ITEM NO. OR TRANS. CODE	DATE	TRANSACTION DESCRIPTION	SUBTRACTIONS AMOUNT OF PAYMENT OR WITHDRAWAL (-)		(-) FEE IF ANY	ADDITIONS AMOUNT OF DEPOSIT OR PAYMENT(+)		BALANCE	
								823	55
	5/14	ATM withdrawal	100	00	.75			100 722	75 80
442	5/16	Ingrid Haupt rent	450	00				450 272	00 80
443	5/18	12th Street Organic Market	12	00				12 260	00 80
	5/28	Deposit				935	52	935 1196	52 32
	6/10	Interest				1	57	1 1197	57 89

4. A. On May 18, there was $260.80 in the account.
   B. On May 18, there was $935.52 in the account.
   C. On May 18, there was $823.55 in the account.
   D. On May 18, the person made a deposit to the account.

5. A. The person paid the rent in cash.
   B. The person paid the rent by check.
   C. The person made an ATM withdrawal to pay the rent.
   D. Ingrid Haupt paid rent to the person.

4. Ⓐ Ⓑ Ⓒ Ⓓ

5. Ⓐ Ⓑ Ⓒ Ⓓ

Name ______________________ ID ____________ Date ____________

Unit 10

Choose an answer.

Rawlins PLUMBING — **Medical Plan Enrollment/Change Application**

Employee Last Name *Pcholkin* First Name *Boris*

30 Thompson St., New Haven, CT 06511 Birth Date *11* *07* *60*
address city state zip m d y

Sex Male [X] Female [ ] Marital Status single [ ] married [X] separated [ ] divorced [ ]

Eligible Dependents	Birth Date (m/d/y)	Sex (M/F)	Relationship
Natasha Pcholkin	*03/09/61*	*F*	*wife*

Boris Pcholkin *October 5, 2003*
employee signature date

1. A. Mr. Pcholkin is not married.
   B. Mr. Pcholkin has one dependent.
   C. Mr. Pcholkin has one child.
   D. Mr. Pcholkin is unemployed.

2. A. Mr. Pcholkin enrolled his wife on November 7.
   B. Mr. Pcholkin enrolled his wife on March 9.
   C. Mr. Pcholkin enrolled his wife on July 11.
   D. Mr. Pcholkin enrolled his wife on October 5.

1. Ⓐ Ⓑ Ⓒ Ⓓ

2. Ⓐ Ⓑ Ⓒ Ⓓ

Marina Lado		Check #	27005
Pay Date	3/7/03	Pay Period	2/19/03-3/5/03 (biweekly)

EARNINGS		DEDUCTIONS	AMOUNT
Gross Pay	$480.00	Federal Tax	$65.30
Net Pay	$372.55	State Tax	$42.15
		Medical Insurance	$0.00
		Total Deductions	$107.45

YEAR-TO-DATE	AMOUNT
Earnings:	$2,405.50
Deductions:	$538.48

Statement Of Earnings ▾ Detach at perforation below and keep for your records ▾

3. What is the pay period for this paycheck?
   A. March 7, 2003.
   B. February 19 to March 5.
   C. July 3, 2003.
   D. March 5 to March 7.

4. What are the total deductions from Ms. Lado's pay this year?
   A. $2,405.50
   B. $538.48
   C. $480.00
   D. $107.45

5. What does Ms. Lado have to pay?
   A. Federal tax and medical insurance.
   B. Federal tax only.
   C. State and federal taxes.
   D. Federal and state taxes and medical insurance.

3. Ⓐ Ⓑ Ⓒ Ⓓ

4. Ⓐ Ⓑ Ⓒ Ⓓ

5. Ⓐ Ⓑ Ⓒ Ⓓ